WITHDRAWN

Big Book
Of Folder Games
for the Innovative Classroom

WITHDRAWN

Big Book Of Folder Games

for the Innovative Classroom

Elaine Commins, M.Ed.

HUMANICS LEARNING
P.O. Box 7400
Atlanta, GA 30357

HUNTINGTON CITY-TOWNSHIP
PUBLIC LIBRARY
200 W. Market Street
Huntington IN 46750

HUMANICS LEARNING

HUMANICS LEARNING
P.O. Box 7400
Atlanta, GA 30357

First Printing 1990

Copyright 1990 Humanics Limited

All rights reserved. No part of this book may be reproduced or used in any form or by any means-graphic, electronic, or mechanical, including photocopying, recording, taping, or information storage and retrieval systems-without written permission of the publishers.

PRINTED IN THE UNITED STATES OF AMERICA

Library of Congress Cataloging- in- Publication Data

Commins, Elaine.
  The Big Book of Folder Games for the Primary Classroom / Elaine Commins.

1.Educational games. 2.Creative activities and seat work.
3.Education, Primary - Curricula. I.Title.
LB1029.G3C66 1989 372.13'97 87-31203
ISBN 0-89334-113-4

Table Of Contents

Chapter 4
Mathematics

Chapter 5
Science

Chapter 6
Social Studies

Big Book Of Folder Games

Implementation

The file folders described in this book are not designed to be kept on a toy shelf for children to use indiscriminately. They are designed to be used in a prescribed manner in order to increase their appeal and entertainment value as well as promote intellectual development. The following method is suggested:

1. Folder games may be offered daily or two or three times a week during work period or free period.

2. No more than two, three or four folder games should be presented to the class at each day's offering. They should be placed on a special small table or at one end of a large work table.

3. Directions for their implementation should be given to the entire class prior to their use. This encourages voluntary participation.

4. Variety is the key to their successful use. Thus, each day's offering should be different. For example, one day's folders might all contain rhyming activities. On another day, they might all be number matching exercises. On still another day they might be devoted to a science project.

5. A sign-up sheet placed on the work table accompanying the folders encourages continuing student participation.

Big Book Of Folder Games

Introduction

Primary grade students are fascinated by games, puzzles, exercises and projects. Here's the opportunity for teachers to add some fun and entertainment to their classrooms by introducing file folders games in an organized manner.

Elaine Commins

Chapter 1

Planning And Preparing

Using the ideas found in this book, teaching can be made easier by providing students with a variety of high interest activities which require very little supervision. The following suggestions are made in order to assist teachers in the optimum use of file folder activities:

1. It is suggested that a special area such as a small work table be used for file folder activities. If possible, each day's presentation of file folders should be correlated in terms of subject matter and operating procedures.

2. Continuing student participation may be encouraged through sign-up sheets. For example, as students finish the activity in a file folder, they sign the sheet. This provides the incentive to begin work on another file folder.

Three different types of sign-up sheets are illustrated here.

A. Each child's name is listed on this sign-up sheet. As children finish a game, they place a check next to their names. Sheets such as this may be mimeographed and changed daily.

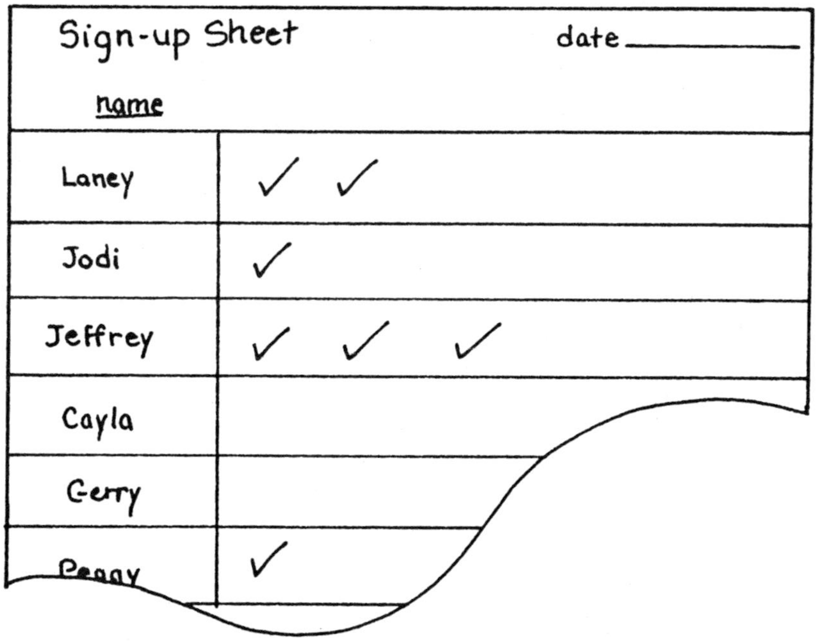

Sign-up Sheet	date _____
name	
Laney	✓ ✓
Jodi	✓
Jeffrey	✓ ✓ ✓
Cayla	
Gerry	
Peggy	✓

B. This second sign-up sheet contains vertical columns. A small illustration at the top of each column identifies specific file folders that are offered on one day. Children sign their names in the proper column upon completion of the task.

12

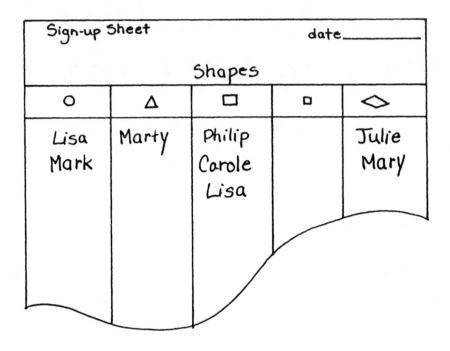

C. The following sheet is used only for competitive games.

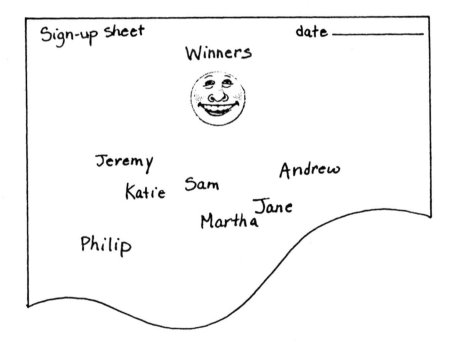

3. If at all possible, file folders should be laminated before they are presented to the children. This prolongs their usability and offers a more professional appearance.

Note: File folders that contain components made of felt should not be laminated.

4. Many file folder activities require small auxiliary parts. These may be stored in zip-lock plastic bags and attached to the file folder with paper clips or clothes pins.

Another method is to prepare a pocket somewhere on the file folder for holding pieces.

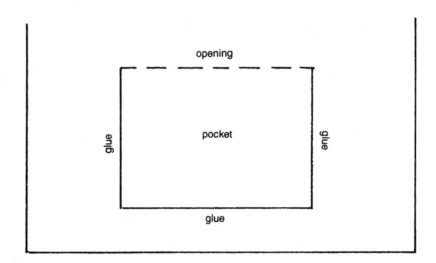

Oak tag is preferred when constructing a pocket. Three sides of the pocket are glued to the file folder. Scotch tape may then be used to reinforce the three glued sides.

If the file folder is to be laminated, the pocket should be attached first. The opening may then be slit with a knife after lamination.

5. By using various colored file folders, a more attractive presentation is made.

6. A collection of junk material is often helpful when preparing file folder activities. Items such as old pre-primers, Weekly Readers, Scholastic, wallpaper books, felt pieces, old magazines, gummed shapes, etc. are suggested.

In addition, teachers who wish to supplement curriculum studies with file folder exercises might consider cutting up current workbooks.

7. When preparing folder games, use water color markers. Permanent markers bleed through to the reverse side.

Chapter 2

Art and Visual-Motor Activities

Beginning with puzzles that develop eye-hand coordination, other skills are emphasized such as drawing and coloring. An introduction into art and famous paintings is offered.

LION PUZZLE

Directions for making puzzle

1 The name of the activity is placed on the cover page.

2 A pocket is constructed on the left center page to hold puzzle pieces.

3 The outline of a lion is traced and cut out of oak tag or posterboard.

4 BEFORE cutting the lion into puzzle pieces, it is traced on the right center page of the folder. (Puzzle shapes may or may not be drawn on the file folder lion.)

5 If possible, laminate the folder and the puzzle pieces.

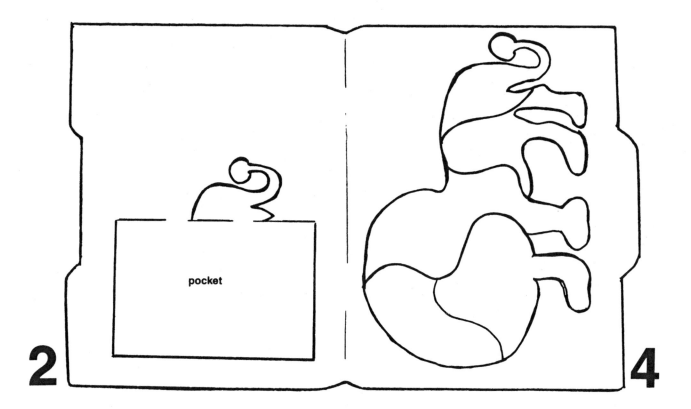

pocket

Directions for use

1. Children place puzzle pieces on the outline.

Suggestion: *Several file folders with animal outlines may be offered at the same time with a sign-up sheet.*

Other suitable subjects for puzzles might include: fruit, vegetables, clothing, toys, trees, maps, automobiles, space ships, etc.

Four animal patterns and a sample sign-up sheet are given on the following pages.

Pattern for LION PUZZLE

Pattern for CAMEL PUZZLE

Pattern for GORILLA PUZZLE

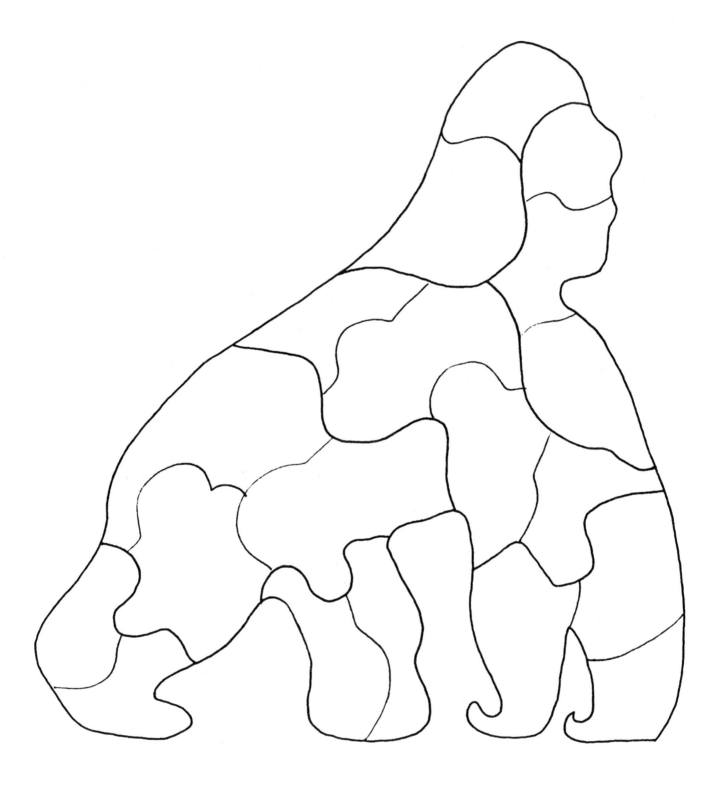

Pattern for ELEPHANT PUZZLE

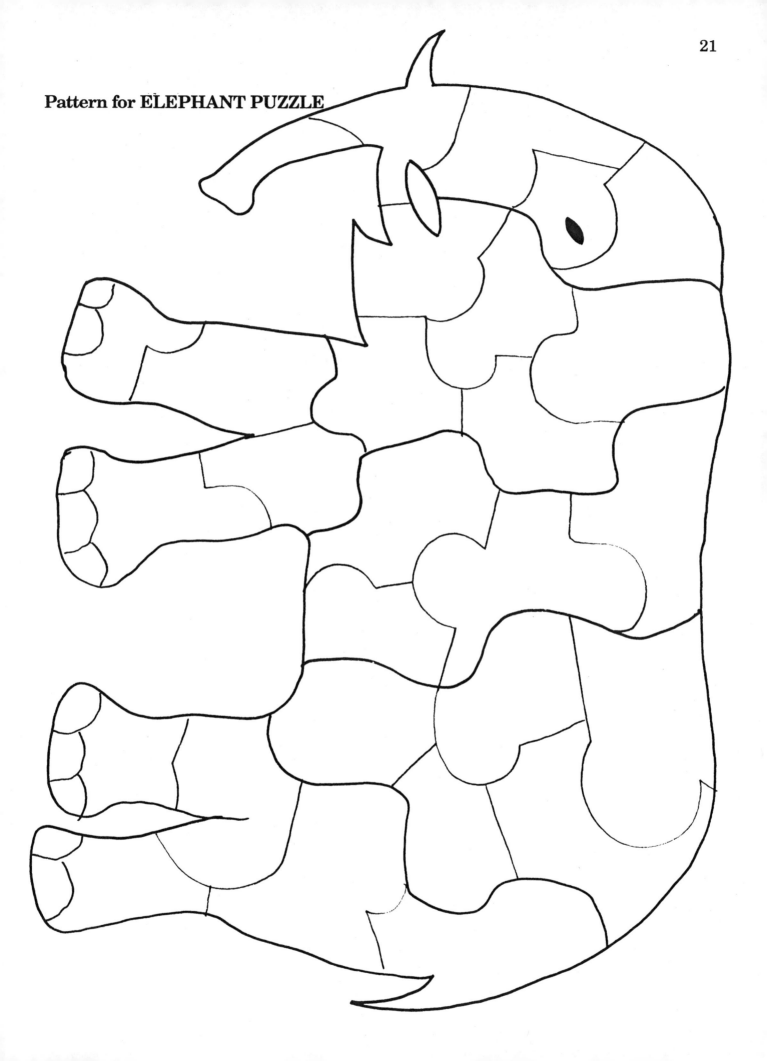

Sample sign-up sheet for animal puzzles

JIGSAW GAME–For 2 Players

Directions for making puzzle

1. The name of the game is placed on the cover page.

2. A colorful picture or design is drawn on the center pages. Puzzle shapes are drawn on the design.

3 Using oak tag, an identical puzzle is drawn and its pieces cut out.

4 The file folder is laminated, as is the identical puzzle, before being cut out.

5 A pocket is constructed on the back page to hold puzzle pieces.

6 A 3-minute egg timer is needed for play.

1

2

Directions for play

1. Puzzle pieces are placed on the table near the playing board.

2. Players take turns picking the top puzzle piece and placing it in its proper position on the board. The egg timer is used to be sure puzzle pieces are positioned within three minutes.

3. If a puzzle piece is not positioned within the allotted time, play is given to the second player.

4. Players may keep a check list when they position a puzzle piece within the time.

3

COPY THE DRAWING

Directions for making activity

1 The name of the activity is placed on the cover page.

2 A grid is drawn on the right center page. A picture is drawn on the grid.

3 The file folder is then laminated.

4 Worksheets containing a similar sized grid–in this instance 3″ x 7″–are provided, along with pencils and crayons.

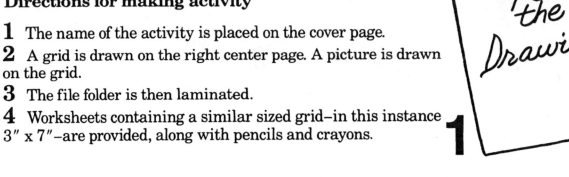

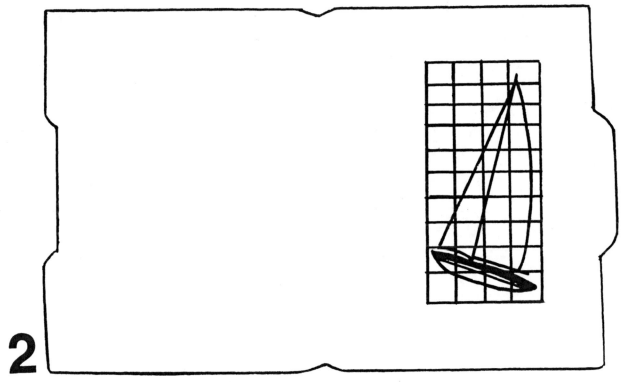

Directions for use

1. Children copy the drawing on their worksheets by carefully matching the drawing in each square.

Suggestion: *Drawings such as this might be coordinated to enhance unit studies such as a drawing of an astronaut, a space ship or a rocket. Several file folders with drawings may be displayed at the same time.*

Worksheet for COPY THE DRAWING

Name_____

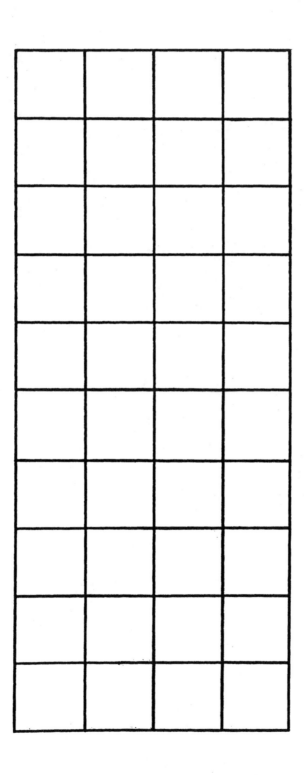

MOOD PICTURES

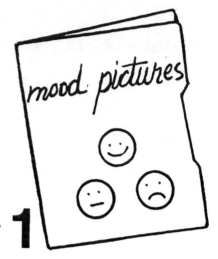

Directions for making activity

1 The name of the activity is placed on the cover page.
2 A series of various colored clouds is drawn on the center pages. Each color represents a different mood.
3 The file folder is laminated.
4 Paper and either paint, crayons or felt markers are provided.

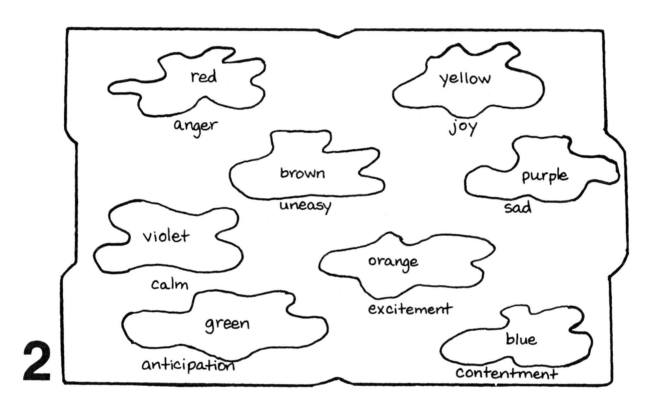

Directions for use

1. Children are asked to draw a picture expressing emotions by using the colors indicated. A class discussion following the project is recommended.

TRACE AND COLOR

Directions for making activity

1 The name of the activity is placed on the cover page.
2 A design (8½″ x 11″) is drawn on the right center page with a heavy, black felt marker.
3 The file folder is then laminated.
4 Typing paper, crayons and pencils are provided.

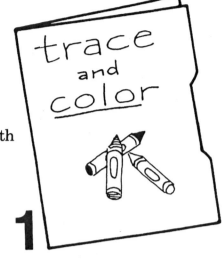

Directions for use

1. A piece of typing paper is placed over the design and the child traces it with a pencil. The tracing may then be colored.

Suggestion: *Several file folders with different patterns to trace and color may be offered to students at the same time. A sign-up sheet may be placed on the table to encourage participation in more than one file folder activity.*

Pattern for TRACE AND COLOR

COLOR BY NUMBERS

Directions for making activity

1 The name of the activity is placed on the cover page.

2 A list of various colors, each numbered, is placed on the left center page.

3 A drawing with clearly defined, numbered areas is placed at the right center page.

4 A worksheet with the same drawing (but minus the numbers) is provided.

5 The file folder is laminated.

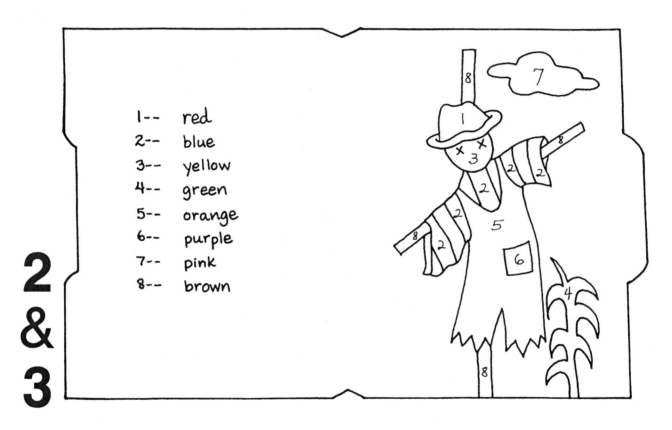

1-- red
2-- blue
3-- yellow
4-- green
5-- orange
6-- purple
7-- pink
8-- brown

Directions for use

1. Children color the worksheet according to the numbered colors, as indicated on the file folder drawing.

Suggestion: *Several file folders with numbered drawings and coordinated worksheets may be offered at the same time.*

Worksheet for COLOR BY NUMBERS

Name_____

Worksheet for COLOR BY NUMBERS

Name_____

Worksheet for COLOR BY NUMBERS

Name_____

Worksheet for COLOR BY NUMBERS

Name_____

HUNTINGTON CITY-TOWNSH
PUBLIC LIBRARY
200 W. Market Street
Huntington IN 46750

NAME THE ARTIST AND THE PAINTING

Directions for making activity

1 The name of the activity is placed on the cover page.

2 A series of numbered paintings is pasted on the center pages. Small, inexpensive copies of famous paintings can usually be purchased at artists' supply stores, book stores or museums.

3 A worksheet with numbered lines is provided.

4 The file folder is then laminated.

Directions for use

1. The child writes the artist's name and the title of the painting on the corresponding number of a worksheet.

Suggestion: *Several file folders devoted to artists and their paintings may be offered. Each may focus on a single school of painting, such as French painters, American painters, Dutch painters, etc. Or they may concentrate on styles of painting such as Impressionism or Realism.*

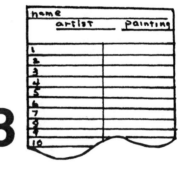

BUTTERFLIES

Directions for making activity

1 The name of the activity is placed on the cover page.

2 Directions are printed on the left center page.

3 A pocket is constructed on the right center page to hold butterfly patterns.

4 Students are given 9 x 12 colored construction paper, pencils, scissors and colored cellophane or tissue paper.

1 butterflies

2 & 3

Directions

1. Fold your paper in half.

2. Place the butterfly pattern on the paper with the body touching the fold.

3. Cut it out. (Do not cut the fold.)

4. Mount it on cellophane or colored tissue paper.

pocket

Directions for use

1. The student folds a piece of colored construction paper in half. The body of the butterfly pattern is place on the fold and then traced and cut out. The student is directed not to cut along the fold.

2. The butterfly is then mounted on colored cellophane or tissue paper. Butterflies may be placed in a window as a spring decoration.

■ A butterfly pattern is given on the following page.

38

Butterfly pattern

place this edge on the fold

EASTER EGGS

Directions for making activity

1 The name of the activity is placed on the cover page.

2 Directions are printed on the left center page.

3 A pocket is constructed on the right center page to hold egg patterns.

4 Students are given manila paper, paint, brushes, pencils, scissors, rubber cement and large cardboard egg patterns.

5 Large cardboard oval patterns are made by the teacher in advance.

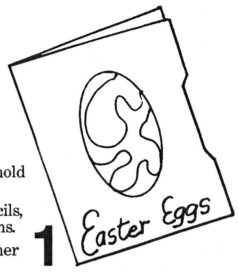

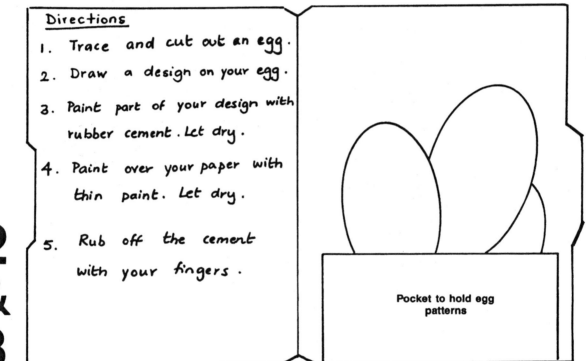

Directions

1. Trace and cut out an egg.
2. Draw a design on your egg.
3. Paint part of your design with rubber cement. Let dry.
4. Paint over your paper with thin paint. Let dry.
5. Rub off the cement with your fingers.

Pocket to hold egg patterns

Directions for use

1. The student traces and cuts out an egg pattern on manila paper. A design is drawn on the egg.

2. Using a small brush, the student paints over portions of the design with rubber cement. It is allowed to dry for 15 minutes.

3. Using a wash of either colored ink or paint, it is brushed over the entire paper and allowed to dry.

4. Using fingertips, the student rubs off the rubber cement.

SNOWFLAKES

Directions for making activity

1 The name of the activity is placed on the cover page.

2 Directions are printed on the left center page.

3 A pocket is constructed on the right center page to hold circle patterns.

4 Pencils, typing paper, scissors, colored cellophane or tissue paper and large cardboard circle patterns are provided.

5 The cardboard circle patterns are constructed in advance by the teacher. They should amost cover a sheet of typing paper.

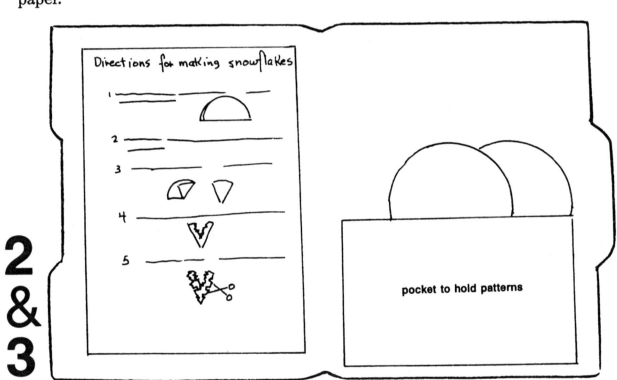

Directions for use

1. The student traces and cuts out a large circle on a sheet of typing paper. Then following the directions for folding, the student snips small cuts out of the folded circle.

2. The snowflake may then be mounted on colored cellophane or tissue paper and taped on a window.

■ Directions for making the snowflake pattern is given on the following page.

Directions for Making Snowflakes

1. Trace and cut out a large circle on typing paper.
2. Fold the circle in half.

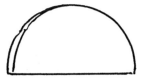

3. Now fold it into 1/3s so that it resembles a triangle with one rounded edge.

4. Using scissors cut an irregularly shaped V out of the rounded edge.

5. Then cut smaller shapes out of the other two sides.

6. Unfolded, it will become a 6-pointed snowflake. It can be mounted on colored cellophane or tissue paper and hung in windows as a winter decoration.

Each snowflake will be different.

■ This sheet may be duplicated and pasted on the left center page of the file folder, or it may be copied by hand.

Chapter 3

Reading

Reading activities in this chapter include a variety of exercises which emphasize basic skills such as identifying synonyms, antonyms, and homonyms. Further identification activities include alphabetizing, finding parts of speech, syllables and searches.

In addition, there are creative projects which encourage writing descriptive as well as narrative paragraphs.

ODD BALLS

Directions for making activity

1 The name of the activity is placed on the cover page.

2 The left center page is labelled "YES" and the right center page is labelled "NO."

3 A series of balls (circles) is prepared in advance by the teacher. Each contains a pair of either matched or mismatched shapes.

   Circles should be laminated before use.

Directions for use

1. The student places all the matched balls on the "YES" page and all the mismatched, or Oddballs, on the "NO" page.

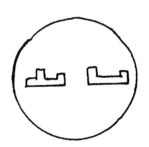
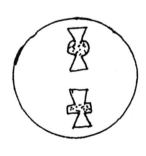

ALPHABET RUN

Directions for making activity

1 The name of the activity is placed on the cover page.

2 Various alphabet runs followed by a blank underlined space are printed on the two center pages.

1

2

lmno____

qrst__

fghi __

defg__

hijKl____

tuvw____

opq____

bcde____

vwxy__

pqr_____

stuv____

jKlm____

klmn____

uvwx____

3 A pocket is constructed on the back page to hold letters.

pocket to hold letters

3

Directions for use

1. The student places the "next" letter on each alphabet run.

TRACING FUN–Cursive

Directions for making activity

1 The name of the activity is placed on the cover page.
2 Five rows of cursive-type writing exercises are placed on the right center page. Arrows should be drawn to indicate starting points.
3 The file folder is then laminated.
4 Tracing paper and pencils are provided.

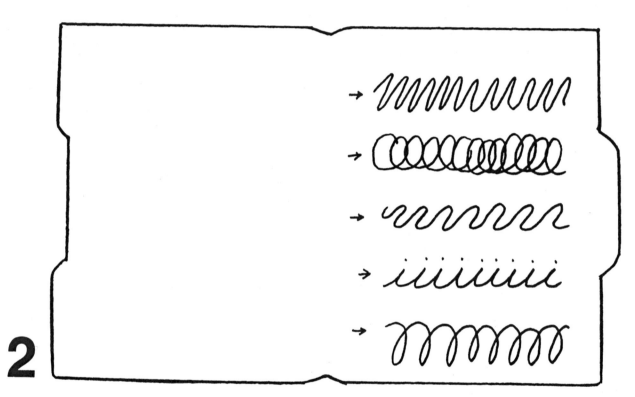

Directions for use

1. Children place tracing paper over the pattern and follow the arrows when they begin tracing.

TRACING FUN–Finish The Line

Directions for making activity

1 The name of the activity is placed on the front cover.

2 Five lines are drawn on the right center page. The beginning of a pattern is drawn on each line.

3 The file folder is then laminated.

4 Tracing paper and pencils are provided.

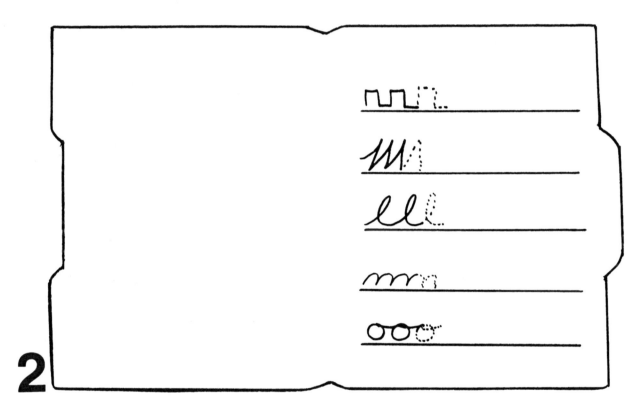

Directions for use

1. Children place tracing paper over the patterns and finish them to the end of the line.[1]

---

[1]Idea for this activity from *Early Childhood* Activities by Elaine Commins, 1982, Humanics Ltd., page 81.

MATCH WORDS TO CONFIGURATION CARDS

Directions for making activity

1 The name of the activity is placed on the cover page. It may be decorated with colored construction paper.

2 Two large pockets are constructed on the center pages. One is labelled "words" and the other "configuration cards."

3 Ten color words on oak tag are constructed with matching blank configuration cards.

4 The file folder is then laminated.

1

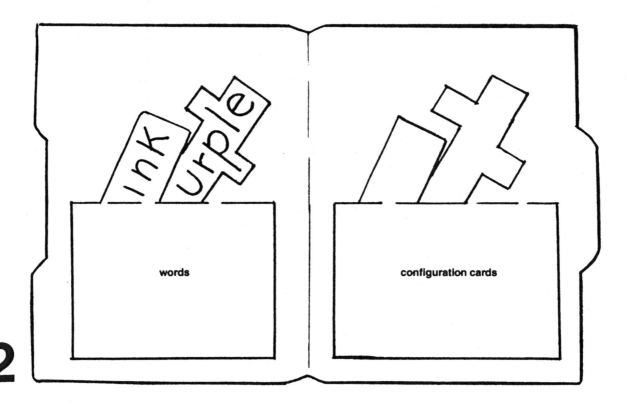

words

configuration cards

2

Directions for use

1. The children remove the cards from their pockets and place matching pairs together.

Instructions for making the cards and a sign-up sheet are given on the next pages.

Suggestion: Several folder games using this same idea may be placed on the table at the same time with a sign-up sheet. Other categories might include: fruit, vegetables, toys, furniture, animals, etc.

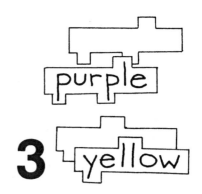

3

Patterns for MATCH WORDS TO CONFIGURATION CARDS

1 The word is printed on oak tag or poster board. Then, using a ruler, the word is outlined.

2 The word is cut out along with a matching blank card. The blank card is the configuration card.

1 purple

2

51

Sign-up sheet for MATCH WORDS TO CONFIGURATION CARDS

colors	fruit	pets	toys

ALPHABETS

RUSSIAN

Directions for making activity

1 The name of the activity is placed on the cover.
2 The Russian (cyrillic) alphabet is printed on the center pages.
3 Paper and marking pens are provided.

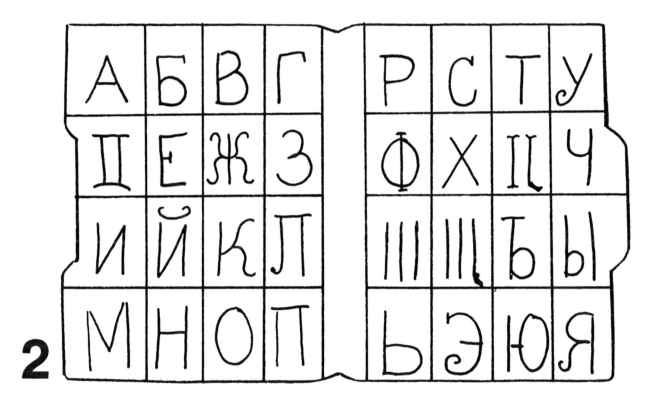

Directions for use

1. Children copy the alphabet on their papers.

2. Several different alphabets may be displayed at one time. If children copy two or more alphabets, they may be stapled into booklets.

On the following pages, several alphabets are provided. They include the Russian (cyrillic), German, Greek, and Hebrew alphabets.

A (ae)   B (b)   V (v)   G (g)

D (d)   (ye)   (zh)   Z (z)

I (ee)   I (ee)   K (k)   L (l)

M (m)   N (n)   O (oh)   P (p)

Russian

Р R (r)	С S (s)	Т T (t)	У Y (oo)
Ф F (f)	Х (kh)	Ц (ts)	Ч (ch)
Ш (sh)	Щ (shch)	Ъ (indicates non-palatalization of preceding consonant)	Ы (ee)
Ь (indicates palatalization of preceding consonant)	Э E (eh)	Ю (eu)	Я (yae)

Russian

A *ah*

E *ah* (eh)

B *bay*

C *tsay*

tsay-hah (kh)

D *day*

E *ay* (eh or ai)

F *eff*

G *gay* (g or kh)

H *hah*

I *ee*

K *kah*

L *ell*

M *em*

N *en*

German

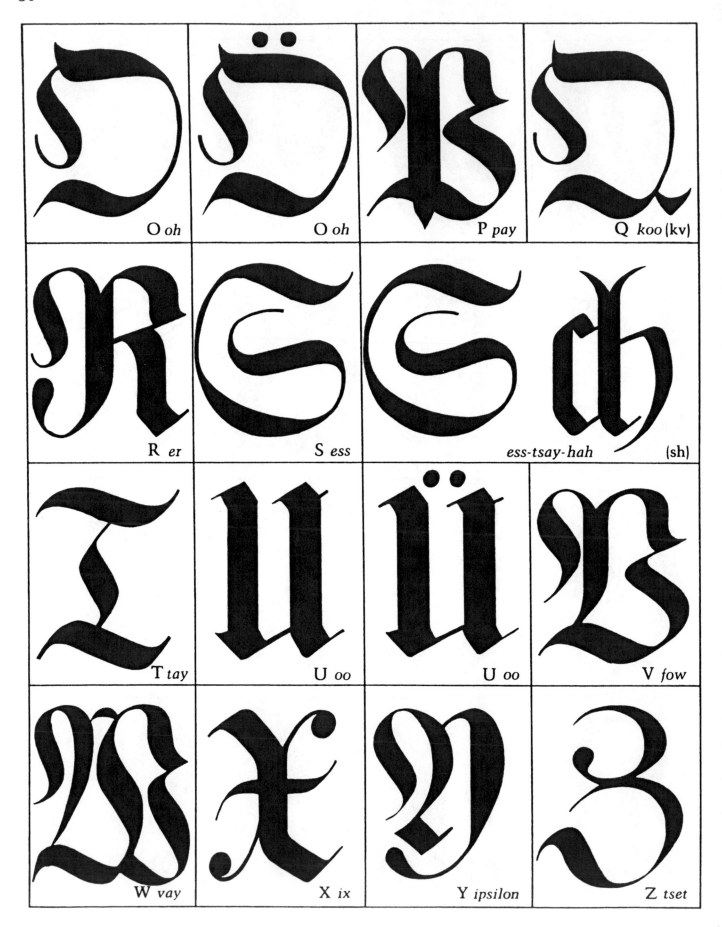

O *oh*

O *oh*

P *pay*

Q *koo* (kv)

R *er*

S *ess*

ess-tsay-hah (sh)

T *tay*

U *oo*

U *oo*

V *fow*

W *vay*

X *ix*

Y *ipsilon*

Z *tset*

German

A *alpha* (ah)

B *beta* (b)

G *gamma* (g)

D *delta* (d)

E *epsilon* (eh)

Z *zeta* (dz)

H *eta* (ey)

theta (th)

I *iota* (ee)

K *kappa* (k)

L *lambda* (l)

M *mu* (m)

Greek

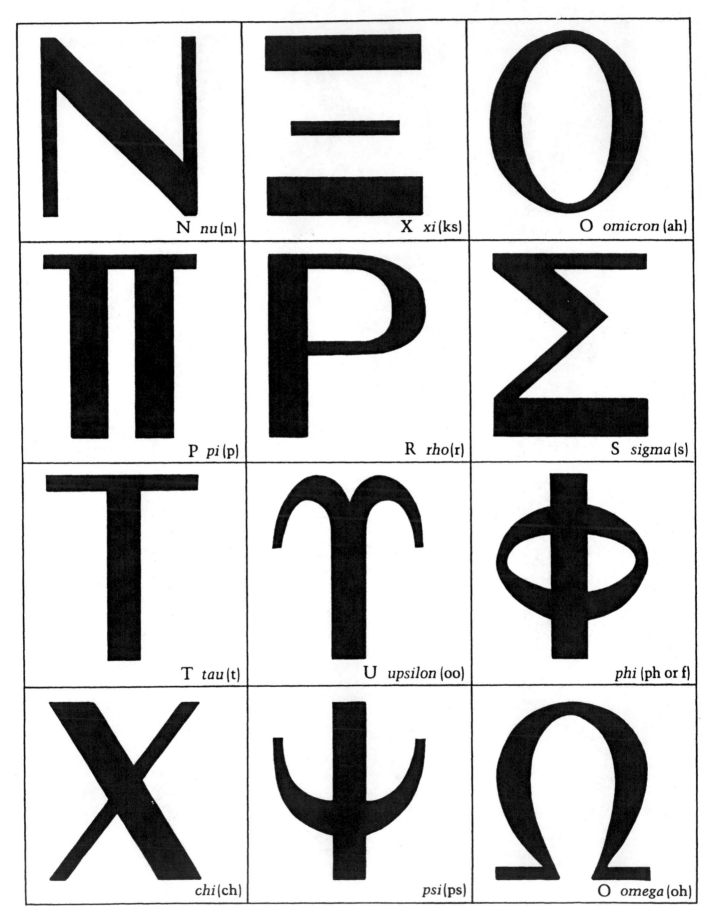

N *nu* (n)

X *xi* (ks)

O *omicron* (ah)

P *pi* (p)

R *rho* (r)

S *sigma* (s)

T *tau* (t)

U *upsilon* (oo)

phi (ph or f)

chi (ch)

psi (ps)

O *omega* (oh)

Greek

Hebrew

N *nun* (n)

(final form used at end of a word)

S *samekh* (s)

(usually silent)

ayin

P *peh* (p)

(final form used at end of a word)

P *peh* (p)

F *feh* (f)

(final form used at end of a word)

F *feh* (f)

tsadi (ts)

(final form used at end of a word)

tsadi (ts)

K *koph* (k)

R *resh* (r)

S *sin* (s)

shin (sh)

T *tav* (t)

thav (th)

Hebrew

SYNONYMS–House

Directions for making activity

1 A house is drawn on the cover page. Chimney smoke from the house forms the name, SYNONYMS. It could also be used for ANTONYMS or HOMONYMS.

2 Windows are drawn on the house, then cut out on three sides.

3 A word is printed on each window.

4 By tracing the opened windows on the right center page, matching windows are drawn behind those on the cover.

5 Synonyms are printed on the inner windows.

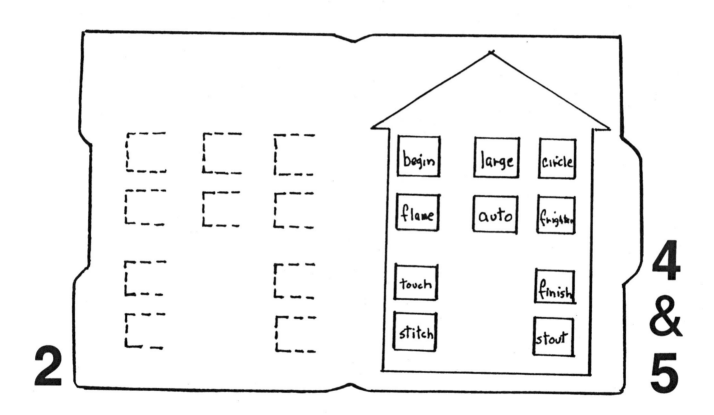

Directions for play

1. The child reads the word on the cover pages, guesses its synonym, then opens the window to check the guess.

Pattern for SYNONYMS HOUSE

SYNONYMS–Word Match

Directions for making activity

1 Colored construction paper is glued on the cover page for decoration. The name of the activity is then printed on with watercolor, felt-tipped markers. Further drawing is suggested.

2 A dozen or more words are printed randomly on the two center pages.

3 An accompanying worksheet lists the synonyms that correspond with the words on the center pages.

4 The file folder is then laminated.

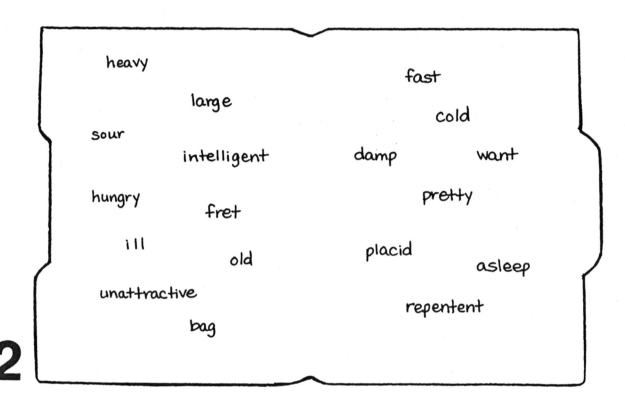

Directions for use

1. Using a worksheet, the child finds the matching word on the file folder and writes it next to its synonym.

64

ANTONYMS

Directions for making activity

1 Scallop-edged, colored construction paper is glued on the cover page. The name of the activity is then printed on with watercolor, felt-tipped markers.

2 A dozen (or more) words are printed randomly on the left center page using one color felt-tipped marker.

3 Antonyms are printed randomly on the right center page using a different color.

4 A worksheet containing 12 numbered lines is provided.

5 The file folder is then laminated.

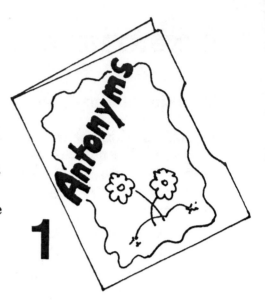

2 & 3

love
dark
frown
come
noisy
hard   soft   far
young   crooked
ugly
dirty   real   sweet
first   last
dull
sharp
rich

poor
last   dull
light   soft
sour   smile   near
hate   beautiful
asleep
spotless   straight
counterfeit
quiet   old
go
sharp   blunt

Directions for use

1. Using the lined worksheets, children write antonym pairs on each line.

4

name _____

1. _____
2. _____
3. _____
4. _____

HOMONYMS

Directions for making activity

1 For decoration, zig-zag cut, colored construction paper is glued on the cover page. The name of the activity is printed on the paper with watercolor, felt-tipped markers.

2 A numbered list of homonyms is printed on the two center pages.

3 A numbered, lined worksheet (or notebook paper) is provided.

4 The file folder is then laminated.

1

2

1. mist, missed
2. through, threw
3. rain, reign
4. sight, site
5. scent, cent
6. flower, flour
7. two, too, to
8. maid, made
9. right, write
10. one, won

11. new, knew, gnu
12. peak, peek
13. for, four
14. blew, blue
15. pair, pear
16. break, brake
17. fair, fare
18. by, buy
19. sleigh, slay
20. night, knight

Directions for use

1. Using a worksheet, the child writes a sentence for each of the numbered homonyms. For example:

1. We missed the boat because of the mist.
7. It is too soon to buy two pounds of cherries.
17. The fare to the fair is one dollar.

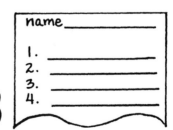

3

INITIAL SOUNDS AND ROOT PHRASES

Directions for making activity

1 The name of the activity is placed on the cover page.

2 A large flower containing eight petals is drawn on each of the center pages. A round, flower-center is attached to each flower by a brad. The brad allows it to be moved. The center contains a root phrase such as: it, in, at, an, ot, ing, ell, etc.

3 A letter (or letters) is written on each petal. Combined with the root phrase, the initial letter forms a word.

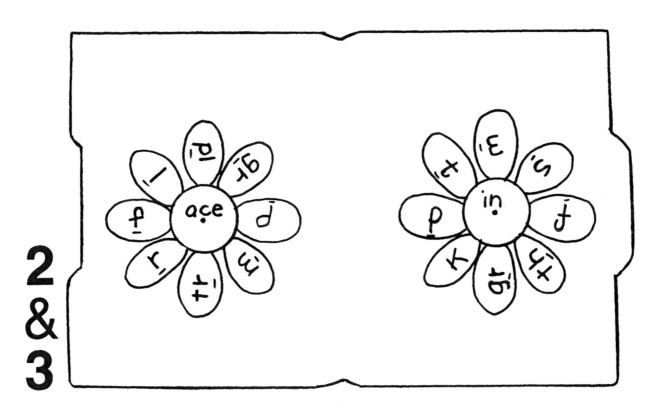

Directions for use

1. By moving the flower center, children line up the root phrase with its initial letter (or letters.) It will form a word. If read correctly to a partner, the child may paste a star next to his/her name on a "Star Sign-up Sheet."

Pattern for INITIAL SOUNDS AND ROOT PHRASES

MIRROR WORDS

Directions for making activity

1 The name of the activity is placed on the cover page. A piece of tinfoil may be pasted on also.

2 The "wrong side" of several words is printed on the center pages. The "wrong side" may easily be obtained by first printing the words with a marking pen on tracing paper and then copying the letters from the reverse side onto the file folder. Words may be outlined.

3 A pocket mirror is needed for use.

4 Paper and pencils are provided.

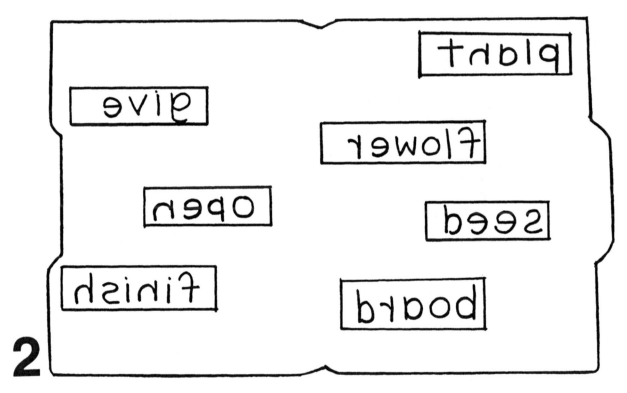

Directions for use

1. Holding the pocket mirror at a perpendicular angle along one side of the word, the child copies it correctly on his/her paper.

Suggestion: Three or four file folders similar to this might be offered at the same time using words found in current curriculum studies. For example, one file folder might contain spelling words, another science words, another history, etc.

Idea adapted from *Bloomin' Bulletin Boards* by Elaine Commins, Copyright, 1984, Humanics Ltd., P.O. Box 7447, Atlanta, Ga. 30309.

NOUNS

Directions for making activity

1 The name of the activity is placed on the cover page.

2 A large circle is drawn on the center pages. It is divided into six segments. A picture is drawn or pasted in each segment. (All the pictures are nouns.)

3 About 1½″ beyond each segment, an angle is cut by using a razor blade. This is to hold matching word-cards.

4. Word-cards that match the pictures are printed and cut out.

5 A pocket is constructed on the back cover to hold the matching word-cards.

1

2 & 3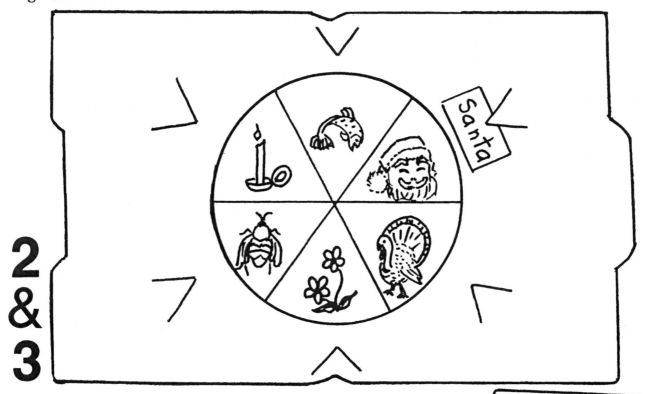

Directions for use

1. Children place the word-cards next to their matching picture under the angle.

4

5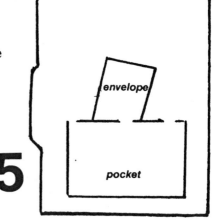

ADD-A-VOWEL

Directions for making game

1 The name of the game is placed on the cover page.

2 A large wheel is drawn on the right center page. It is divided into five segments, each containing a vowel.

3 Specially prepared worksheets must accompany the game. Each worksheet contains 24 words, all with missing vowels.

4 The file folder is laminated before a spinner is attached.

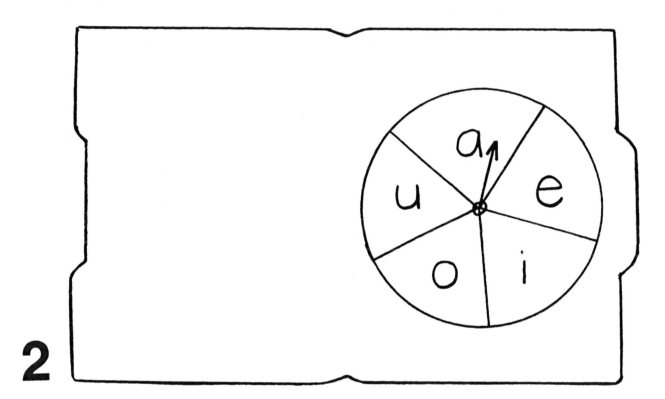

Directions for play

1. Players are given identical worksheets.

2. They take turns spinning. When the arrow lands on a vowel, they fill in one of the blank spaces on their worksheet.

3. If the vowel does not make a word, they forfeit a turn.

4. The first to fill in all the words on the worksheet wins.

The following two worksheets are examples:

Two types of ADD-A-VOWEL worksheets

Name _____ date _____
Add-A-Vowel Worksheet

g__t	f__x	c__d
d__n	d__t	n__t
b__t	c__t	m__d
h__p	f__g	f__n
b__d	h__m	m__b
b__g	h__n	t__g
c__b	d__d	b__s
g__p	d__p	c__p

Name _____ date _____
Add-A-Vowel Worksheet

b__ck	f__st	l__nd
d__ll	l__ck	r__ck
s__ck	b__st	d__mp
dr__p	sh__p	th__n
th__t	h__lp	n__st
b__ss	j__st	p__ck
f__sh	t__ll	s__ng
p__ck	sl__m	s__nk

Winner's worksheet should be checked by the teacher for accuracy. Some kind of reward or recognition such as a star, smiley face, etc. may be given to indicate achievement.

TUNE IN ON NOUNS

Directions for making activity

1 The name of the activity is placed on the cover page.
2 Directions are written on the left center page.
3 A drawing of a record is placed on the right center page. It indicates where the name of the record and the nouns are to be placed on a worksheet.
4 Worksheets accompany the activity.
5 Equipment needed: a record player, headphones and single records with vocalists.

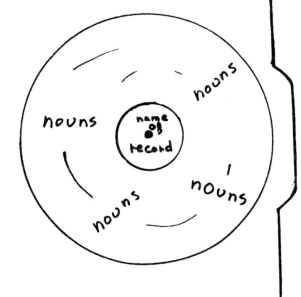

Directions for use

1. Listening to the record, the child writes down all the nouns on the indicated position on the worksheet.

Suggestion: *"Tune In On" activities that use other parts of speech such as verbs and adjectives may also be constructed.*

FISHING FOR VERBS AND ADJECTIVES

Directions for making activity

1 The name of the activity is placed on the cover page.

2 A large fishbowl is drawn on each of the center pages. One is titled VERBS, the other ADJECTIVES.

3 Twenty-five or more fish are cut out. A verb or adjective is printed on each fish.

4 A pocket is constructed on the back cover to hold fish.

1

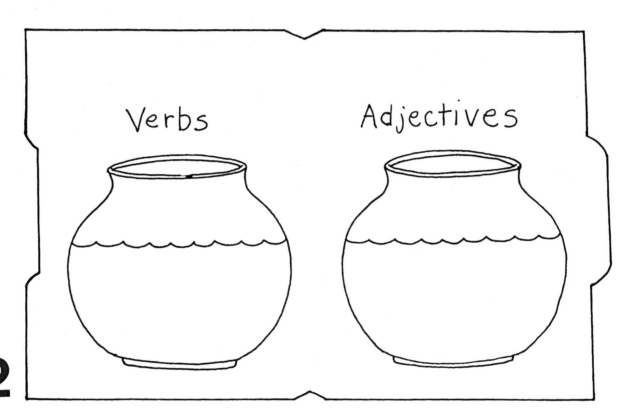

Verbs   Adjectives

2

Directions for use

1. The fish are scrambled and placed near the playing board. They may be kept in a plate. Children take turns placing each fish in the proper bowl.

3

swim

Pattern for FISHING FOR VERBS AND ADJECTIVES

BARRELS OF WORDS GAME

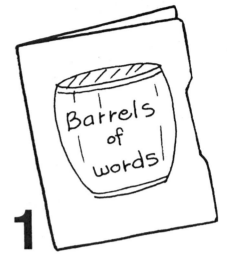

Directions for making game

1 The name of the game is placed on the cover page.

2 Four barrels are drawn on the center pages. One part of speech, either a verb, noun, adjective or adverb, is printed on each barrel.

3 Over 30 numbered sentence strips are prepared by the teacher. One word (either an adjective, verb, noun or adverb) is underlined in each sentence.

4 A pocket is constructed on the back page to hold the sentence cards.

5 For checking, a numbered answer card may be provided and kept in the pocket.

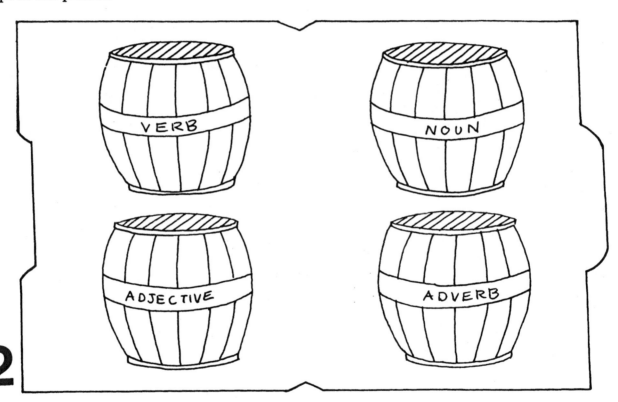

Directions for play

1. Sentence strips are placed face down on the board.

2. From two to four players take turns drawing a strip. They read the sentence aloud and place the strip on the proper barrel.

3. Another player checks the answer. If correct, the player receives a point; if wrong, he/she loses that turn.

4. One player is selected to keep score.

Pattern for BARRELS OF WORDS GAMES

HOW MANY WORDS IN THE MAGIC OVAL?

Directions for making activity

1 The name of the activity is placed on the cover page.
2 A large, sectioned oval is drawn on the center pages.
3 Overlapping words are printed in the sections.
4 Lined paper and pencils are provided.

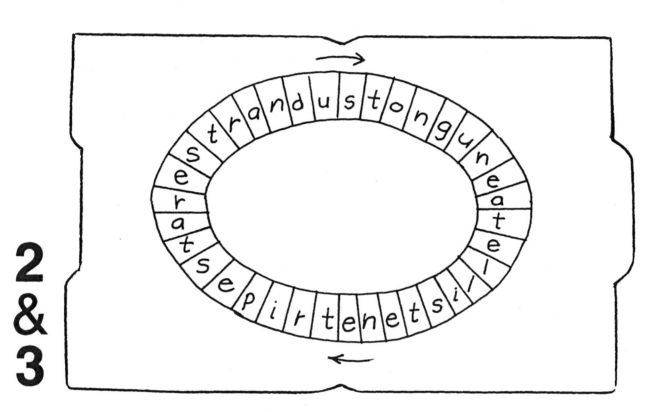

Directions for use

1. The child, following the direction of the arrows, finds and lists as many words as possible on his/her paper. (There are more than 20 words in this oval.)

Suggestion: *Several file folders with magic ovals—each containing different words—may be offered at the same time. Children are encouraged to work as many as possible for credit.*

WORD SEARCH–Things Found in a Schoolroom

Directions for making puzzle

1 The name of the puzzle is placed on the cover page.

2 A grid, 7″ x 8½″, is constructed on the right center page.

3 A single topic is selected such as: Things Found in a School-room, or Things Found on a Playground or Things Found in a Hospital, etc. Items found in the particular topic are printed on the grid either forward, backward or diagonally. The remaining empty spaces may be filled in with miscellaneous letters.

4 Worksheets, containing empty grids, are provided.

1

2 & 3

X	R	E	P	A	P	Y	M
K	C	O	L	C	T	U	W
N	D	A	Z	D	E	S	K
S	R	O	S	S	I	C	S
Q	H	L	O	B	X	G	F
T	C	R	R	R	U	S	K
N	D	J	U	I	T	L	M
I	W	P	X	L	A	Z	Y
A	Y	M	N	H	E	H	O
P	E	N	C	I	L	R	C

Directions for use

1. As the child finds a word on the file folder grid, it is copied on the worksheet grid.

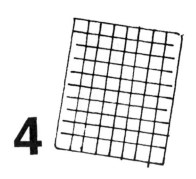

4

Pattern for WORD SEARCH

CHAIN LINKING OPPOSITES

Directions for making activity

1 The name of the activity is placed on the cover page.

2 A list of words is printed on the left center page. The top word has its opposite written next to it. The opposite word will be the first word to be printed in the link.

3 Worksheets with chain links drawn on them are stapled to the right center page.

2 & 3

1. work---play
2. fast
3. no
4. stop
5. sour
6. difficult
7. winter
8. love
9. give
10. succeed

Directions for use

1. The child detaches a worksheet and writes the opposite of each word on the chain link. The last letter of every word becomes the first letter of the next word. There are no spaces between words.

2. Hint: words are not listed in order.

DIAL-A-PLURAL

Directions for making activity

1 A telephone is drawn on the cover page. Nine rectangles, each representing a push button, are cut out of the drawing. Nine singular words are written above the push buttons.

2 Answers may be printed on the inside cover above each push button for children to check their work.

3 Directions are printed on the back cover.

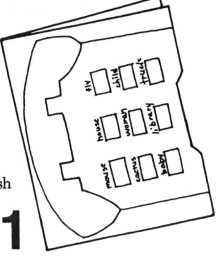

1

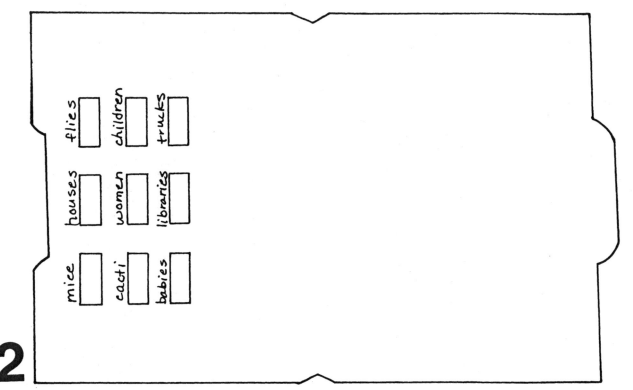

2

Directions for use

1. The child inserts a piece of paper in the folder and writes the plural for each word.

Pattern for DIAL-A-PLURAL

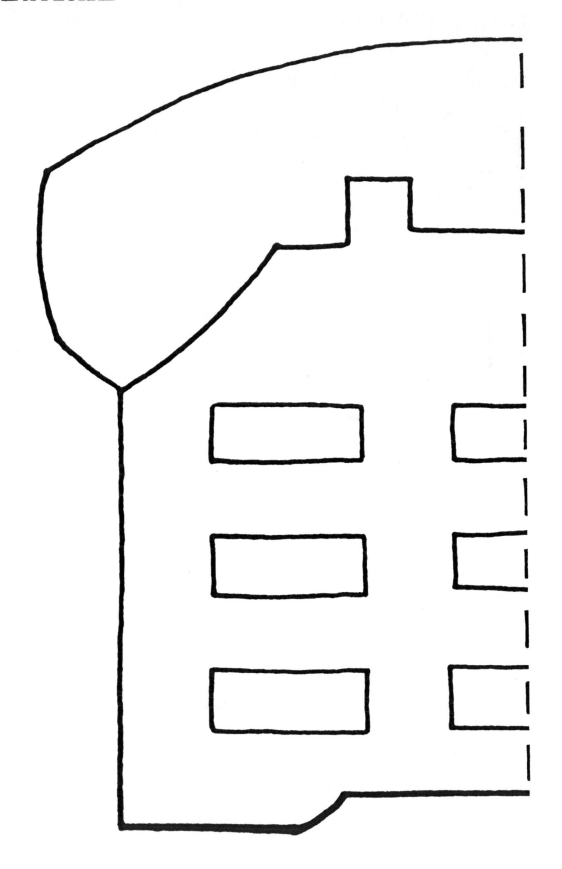

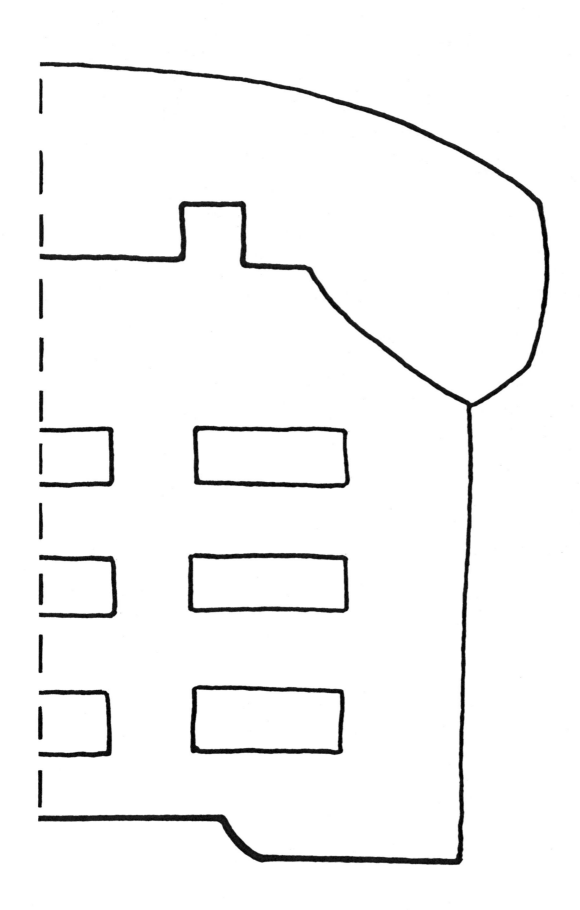

SCRAMBLED WORDS

Directions for making activity

1 The name of the activity is placed on the cover page.
2 Numbered words (taken from spelling lists) are scrambled and printed on the two center pages.
3 Worksheets with numbered lines are provided.

1

2

1. saott
2. bknal
3. dolc
4. resto
5. nerup

6. vesto
7. tigrh
8. calenc
9. cpire
10. relac

Directions for use

1. Children unscramble the words and write each one on the corresponding line of the worksheet. For example:

> *1. toast*
> *2. blank*
> *3. cold*

3

Suggestion: *Several different file folders with numbered worksheet may be offered at the same time. Words may be taken from literature books, science lessons or social studies texts.*

SCRAMBLED LETTERS

Directions for making game

1 The name of the game is placed on the cover page.

2 Two grids, each containing ten spaces, are drawn at each end of the center pages.

3 Alphabet cards, sized to fit spaces on the grid, are prepared. One color is used for vowels, another for consonants. Two complete alphabets plus four additional cards for each vowel are suggested.

4 A pocket is constructed on the back cover to hold the alphabet cards.

5 Paper and pencils are provided.

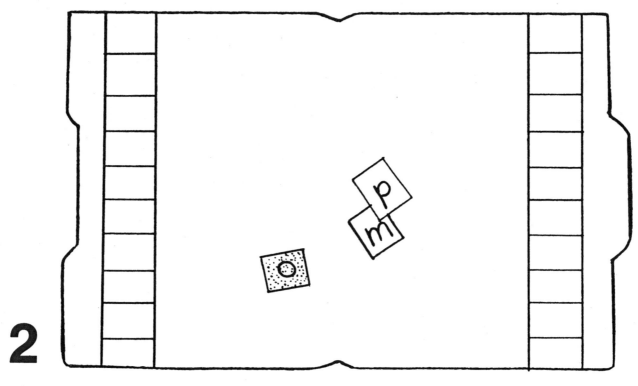

Directions for play

1. Each player selects a grid.

2. Alphabet cards are placed face down on the center of the playing board. Each player selects seven consonants and three vowels and places them on his/her grid.

3. Players jot down as many words as they can form from their letters.

4. The player with the most words wins.

5. Another game may commence using cards from those that are remaining in the center of the board.

TOUCHDOWN WITH COMPOUNDS

Directions for making game

1 The name of the game is placed on the cover page.

2 A football grid is drawn on the center pages. "Home Team" is printed on one end and "Visitors" on the opposite end.

3 Thirty-five word cards are prepared by the teacher. On 20 cards, compound words are printed. On 10 cards, two-syllable words such as tulip or frontier are printed. On 5 cards, the word "penalty" is printed.

4 Two football markers are provided. One is "Home Team," the other "Visitors."

5 An envelope to hold the cards may be attached to the back cover.

6 Directions for play are printed on the back cover.

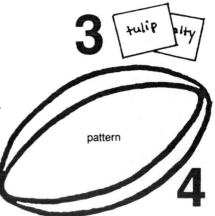

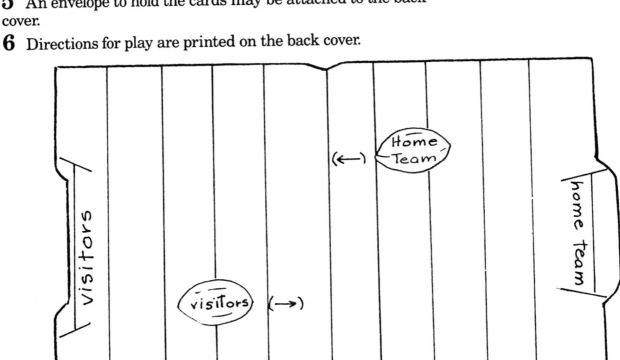

Directions for play

1. Each player selects a football marker.

2. Cards are positioned face down near the grid. Players take turns drawing cards and enter the game on their own ten yard line.

3. If the card shows a compound word, the player moves the football ten yards towards the other team's goal. If the card is not a compound word, the player loses a turn. If the card is a penalty card, the player goes back ten yards.

4. The first player to cross the other team's ten-yard line wins.

5. A check-list of compound words may be provided.

SECRET MESSAGES

Directions for making activity

1. The name of the activity is placed on the cover page.

2 A large telephone dial is drawn on the center pages.

3 Worksheets are prepared to accompany the activity. The first letter of a list of secret words is given. The clues to the remaining letters are indicated by numbered blanks. Each number on the dial contains three letters. The child must select the correct letter to form a word.

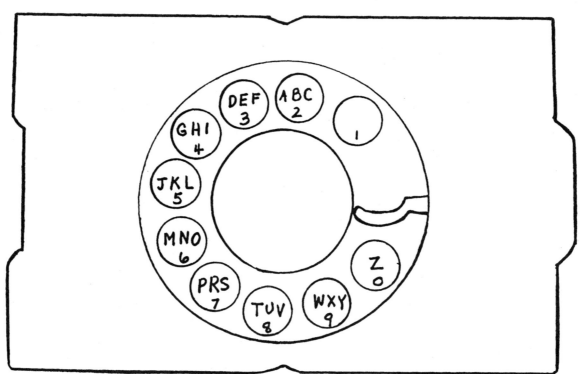

Directions for use

1. After the child selects the correct letter to form a word, the words are then arranged to form a message.

An example of a worksheet for SECRET MESSAGES is given on the following page.

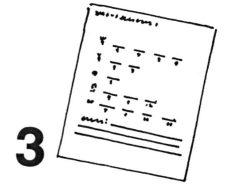

Worksheet for SECRET MESSAGES

W ___ ___ ___ ___ ___
9   4   7   4   3   7

Y ___ ___ ___
9   3   2   7

A
Z

B ___ ___ ___
Z   3   7   8

F ___ ___
3   6   7

H ___ ___ ___ ___
4   2   7   7   9

N ___ ___
6   3   9

The message is: _____

_____

(The answer to this SECRET MESSAGE is: "Best wishes for a happy new year.")

Pattern for SECRET MESSAGES

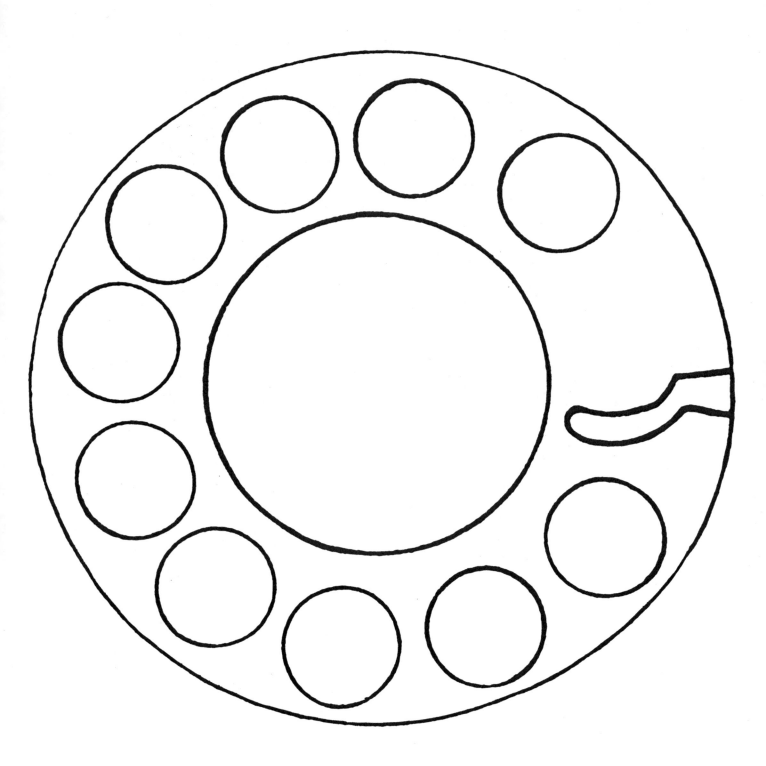

ALPHABETIZING

Directions for making activity

1 The name of the activity is placed on the cover page.
2 Subjects to be listed in alphabetical order are given on the center pages.
3 Paper, pencils and a dictionary are provided.

1

Select one subject to
   ALPHABETIZE

an animal alphabet   book title alphabet

a food alphabet   famous persons alphabet

a plant alphabet   a heavenly alphabet

U.S. cities alphabet   song title alphabet

foreign cities alphabet   automobile alphabet

USE THE DICTIONARY   USE ENCYCLOPEDIAS

2

Directions for use

1. The child selects one of the listed subjects and alphabetizes it. Use of a dictionary and/or encyclopedias is encouraged. For example, if the student selects "animals" as the subject, the following list might be made:

> Ant
> Bear
> Chimpanzee
> Deer
> Elephant
> Giraffe
>   etc.

LITTLE RED RIDING HOOD–
Sequencing

Directions for making activity

1 The name of the story is placed on the cover page.

2 Rectangles, sized to match the pictured rectangles are drawn on the center pages and numbered.

3 Inexpensive fairy tale books are purchased at a drug store or discount store. The pictures are cut out and mounted on oak tag rectangles.

4 A pocket is constructed on the back page to hold pictures.

5 The file folder is then laminated.

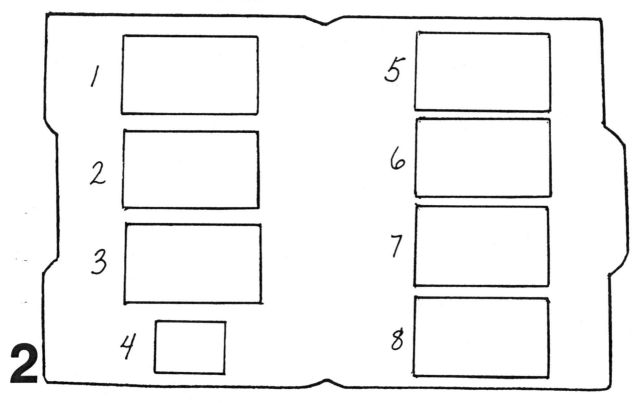

Directions for use

1. The child arranges the pictures in sequence on the numbered rectangles in the center pages.

Suggestion: *Several different fairy tales might be offered at the same time. Children could "read" their stories to each other as they finish sequencing them.*

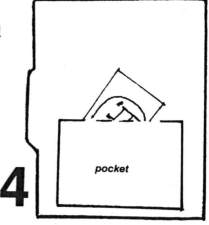

TELL THE STORY

Directions for making activity

1 The name of the activity is placed on the cover page.
2 Four untitled, numbered pictures are drawn or pasted on the center pages.

Suggestion: For use with older children, the story may depict a health related issue such as the one illustrated here. For example, in 1) a child stands in the playground, ignored by peers; 2) the child takes out a large bag of candy; 3) curious children approach the child and 4) most of the children walk away from the child, discussing the potentially harmful effects of eating too much candy; (the need for a balanced diet, dental decay, etc.) .

Directions for use

1. Children may write their responses in essays, or they may use the story in a group discussion. Teachers should lead discussion and also require children to project future consequences.

SHORT STORIES

Directions for making activity

1 The teacher cuts out short stories from children's magazines such as "Cricket," "Jack and Jill," "Highlights," "World," etc. Usually, old copies of these magazines may be obtained from the school librarian.

2 The story and its illustrations are glued on the file folder which is then laminated for durability.

3 In the event that the story is longer than two pages in the magazine, two copies of the same magazine are needed in order to obtain the front and back of each page.

Directions for use

1. The stories may be used for recreational purposes or students may be required to prepare oral or written reports for credit.

Suggestion: *A collection of short stories may be presented to children at specific times or available at any time.*

THE SYL-LA-BLE GAME

Directions for making game

1 The name of the game is placed on the cover page.

2 A sectioned pathway is drawn on the center pages.

3 Word cards are prepared by the teacher. After laminating, they are placed face down on the playing board.

4 Markers are provided.

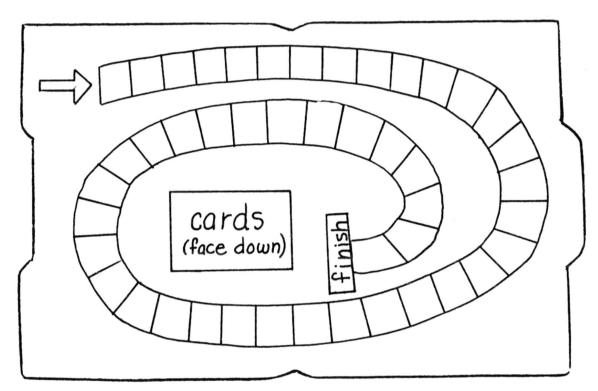

Directions for play

1. Each player selects a marker.

2. Players take turns drawing word cards, then moving their markers as many spaces as the word has syllables.

3. The first player to reach finish, wins.

WORD STEP GAME

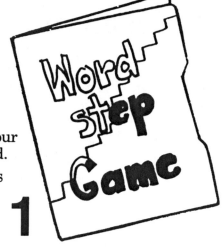

Directions for making activity

1 The name of the activity is placed on the cover page.

2 A grid is drawn on the right center page. It may be three, four or five columns wide. The more columns, the more complicated.

3 A word is printed across the top row and a different word is printed across the bottom row.

4 Paper and pencils are provided.

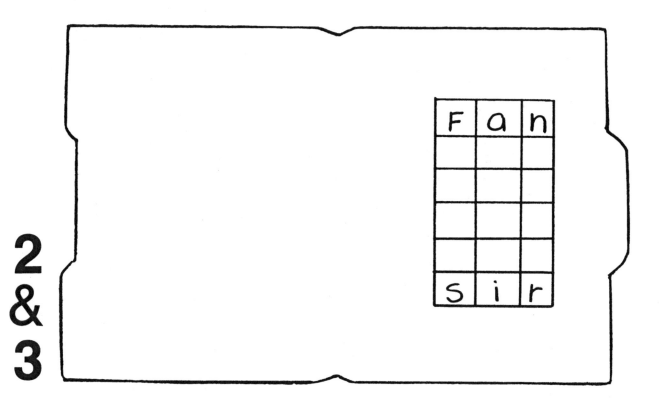

Directions for use

1. Working from top to bottom, the student changes one letter in each row to form a new word until the final printed word is attained. Two examples are given here:

fan	plant
pan	plane
pat	plate
pit	slate
sit	state
sir	stare

STUFFED ANIMALS-Name me

Directions for making activity

1 The name of the activity is placed on the cover page.
2 A paired list of letters is printed on the center pages.
3 Paper and pencils are provided.

Stuffed animals

A. L.
C. B.
T. D.
F. M.
S. W.

Name me

R. X.
E. P.
G. N.
H. V.
J. Y.

Directions for use

1. Students, using the suggested initials, make up names for stuffed animals
For example: A.L. = Agatha Lorraine
        C.B. = Callie Bedelia

PETS-My history

Directions for making activity

1 The name of the activity is placed on the cover page.
2 A list of ten or more questions is placed on the center pages.
3 Lined paper and pencils are provided.

2

Pets - My history

1. My name ?

2. Date and place of birth ?

3. Weight ?

4. Owner(s) name ?

5. Home address ?

6. Where I sleep ?

7. Color ?

8. Favorite food ?

9. My dinnertime ?

10. Favorite activity ?

Directions for use

1. Children answer the questions on their papers.
2. Illustrations are suggested.

TELL-A-TALE

Directions for making activity

1 The name of the specific tale to be used is placed on the cover page.

2 A background picture may be painted on the center pages.

3 Small, paper puppets stapled to popsicle sticks are provided.

4 A pocket is constructed on the back cover to hold puppets.

1

2

Directions for use

1. Several different TELL-A-TALE stories are placed on the table. The teacher selects a story and tells it to the class.

Suggestion: *Other TELL-A-TALE stories might include, "Goldilocks," "The Three Billy Goats Gruff," "The Gingerbread Boy," "Little Red Riding Hood," etc.*

3

pocket

4

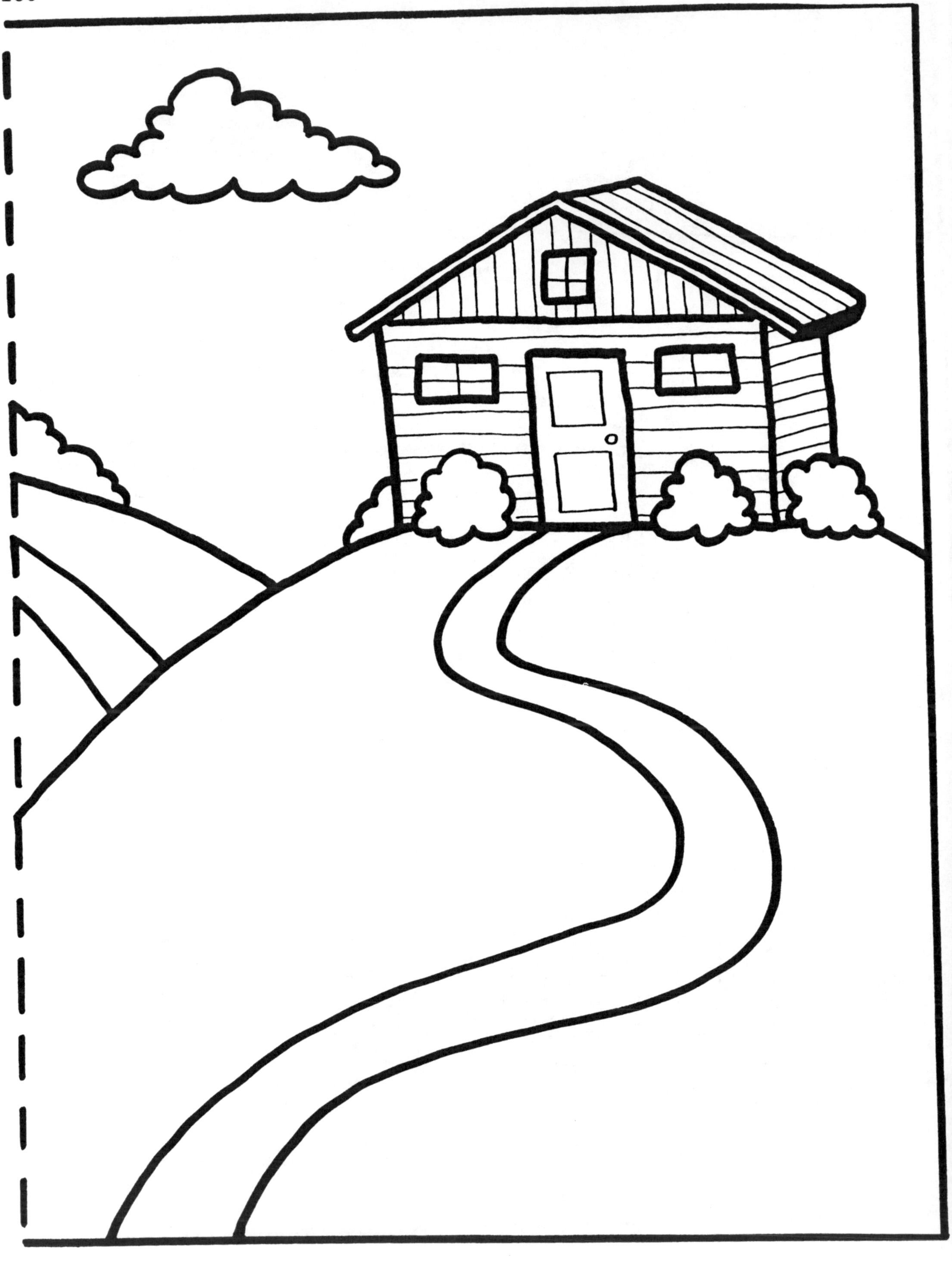

Pattern for TELL-A-TALE puppet

1 Construction paper or oak tag is used. It is folded and, on the fold, a pig is drawn and cut out of the "doubled" paper, making sure not to cut the folded edge.

2 The "doubled" pig is then laminated.

3 A tongue depressor or popsickle stick is inserted in the "doubled" pig, stapled and used as a handle.

Chapter 4

Mathematics

All the math projects presented in this chapter are geared to supplement on-going classroom programs.

Subjects include number games, problems that identify time, coins, exercises with rulers, computers, and telephones. In addition there are folder games that concentrate on addition, subtraction, multiplications, fractions, and word problems.

COVER THE BOARD

Directions for making the game

1 The name of the game is placed on the cover page.

2 A grid is drawn across the two inner pages of the file folder.

3 A die plus a supply of two different colored chips or chits are provided. Each player gets a single-colored supply of chits.

1

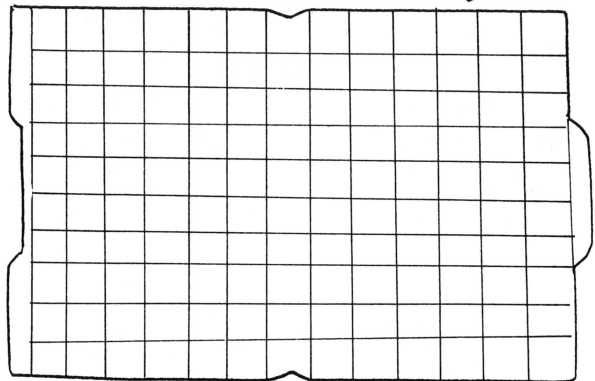

2

4 A pocket is constructed on the back page to hold chits (small squares of colored construction paper.)

3 & 4

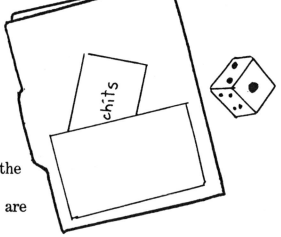

Directions for use

1. Students take turns tossing the die and placing the matching number of chits on the grid.

2. When the board is completely covered, the chits are counted and the one with the most chits wins.

THE SEQUENCE GAME – Two More Than

Directions for making game

1 The name of the game is placed on the cover page.

2 A number line is drawn on the left center page. Below the number line, a circle with a spinner is constructed. Divided into six segments, numbers from three to eight are printed in each segment.

3 A grid is drawn on the right center page. Numbers from five to ten are printed randomly in each space on the grid.

4 Directions for play are printed on the back cover. (Laminate before attaching spinner.)

5 Two sets of different colored chips are needed for play.

2 & 3

| 1 | 2 | 3 | 4 | 5 | 6 | 7 | 8 | 9 | 10 |

two more than

10	6	5	9	7	8
5	8	6	7	10	9
9	10	8	6	5	7
8	5	5	10	8	5
9	7	10	9	7	8
10	8	7	6	9	6

Directions for play

1. Each player chooses a set of colored chips.

2. Players take turns spinning. A chip is placed on a number that is two more than the number indicated on the spinner.

3. The first player to cover all the numbers in one row—either horizontally or vertically—wins.

Suggestion: *Similar games using "less than" may be offered at the same time. One, two or three "more than" or "less than" are acceptable.*

Grid for THE SEQUENCE GAME

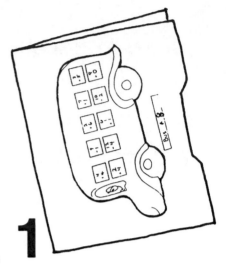

BUS #8–Commutative Property Exercise

Directions for making activity

1 The name of the activity is printed on the cover page along with a drawing of the bus.

2 Ten windows are drawn. They are cut out on three sides in order to "flap" open.

3 Addition or subtraction problems are written on the outside of each window. All problems must have the answer "8."

4 The answers to the problems are written directly behind the windows and are revealed when the windows are opened.

Directions for use

1. Children take turns using this model file folder. A pattern is given on the following page.

2. Children are then given bus worksheets. (See pattern.) They select their own bus number and write problems that equal that number in each window.

Name_____

Worksheet for BUS #8

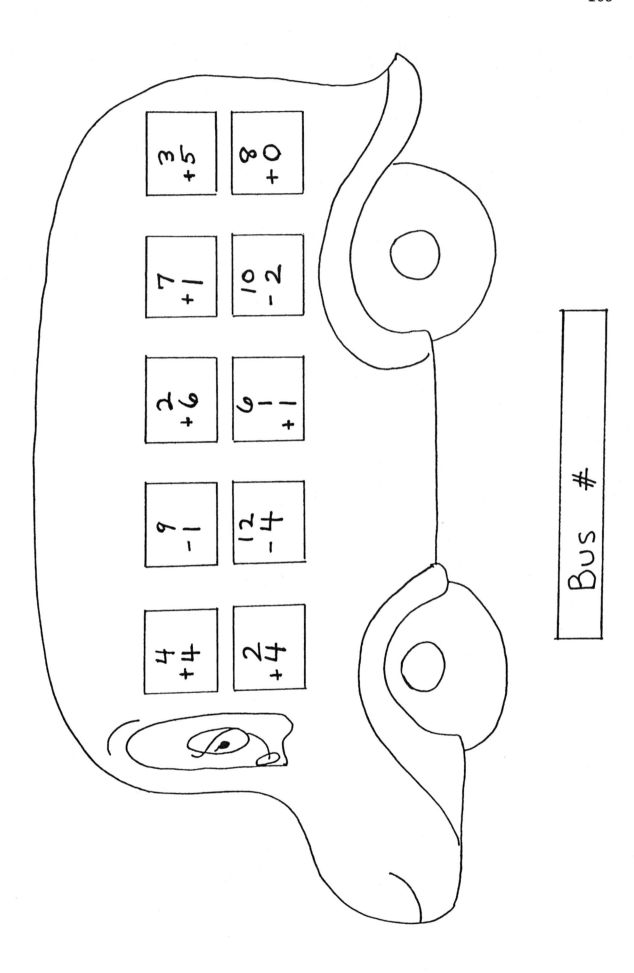

$$\begin{array}{r} 3 \\ +5 \end{array}$$ $$\begin{array}{r} 7 \\ +1 \end{array}$$ $$\begin{array}{r} 2 \\ +6 \end{array}$$ $$\begin{array}{r} 9 \\ -1 \end{array}$$ $$\begin{array}{r} 4 \\ +4 \end{array}$$

$$\begin{array}{r} 8 \\ +0 \end{array}$$ $$\begin{array}{r} 10 \\ -2 \end{array}$$ $$\begin{array}{r} 6 \\ +1 \end{array}$$ $$\begin{array}{r} 12 \\ -4 \end{array}$$ $$\begin{array}{r} 2 \\ +4 \end{array}$$

Bus #

SET THE CLOCKS

Directions for making activity

1 The name of the activity is placed on the cover page.

2 Several clock faces are drawn on the center pages. Under each clock face a specific time is written. The file folder is then laminated.

3 Moveable hands are inserted in each clock face. (These can be purchased.)

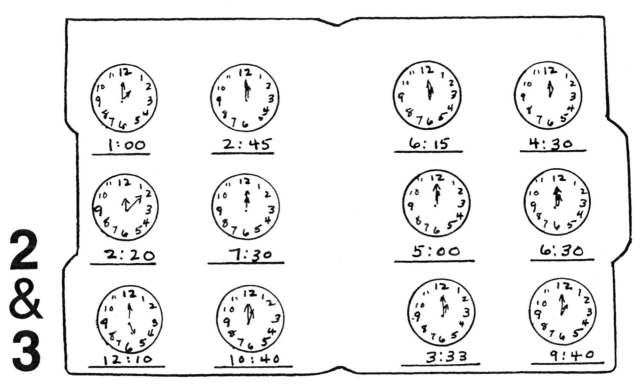

1:00   2:45   6:15   4:30

2:20   7:30   5:00   6:30

12:10   10:40   3:33   9:40

Directions for use

1. The child sets each clock according to the stated time.

WHAT TIME IS IT?

Directions for making game

1 The name of the game is placed on the cover page.

2 About 35 clock faces, each indicating a different time, are drawn on the center pages.

3 Two markers and a wheel with a spinner that is numbered to three are provided.

4 An answer sheet is provided.

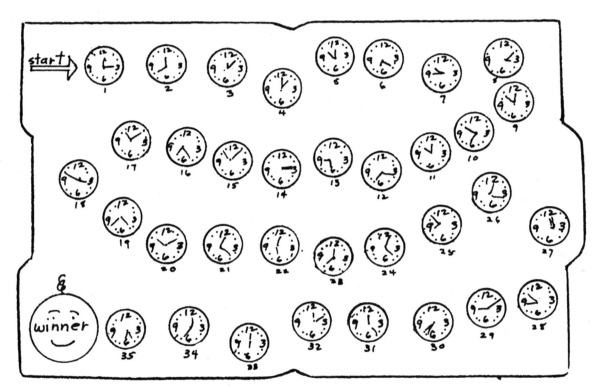

Directions for play

1. Each player selects a marker and then takes turns spinning. As indicated by the arrow, the player moves either one, two or three spaces forward.

2. The player must then tell the correct time on the clock face. If missed, the player goes backward the number of times indicated on the wheel.

3. Answers may be checked on the answer sheet.

COUNTING COINS

Directions for making activity

1 The name of the activity is placed on the cover page.

2 The center pages are divided into several sections and a price tag is drawn in each section. Various prices are written on each price tag.

3 A packet of real or play coins is stapled on the left center page. Pennies, nickels, dimes and possibly quarters should be included–with a preponderance of pennies.

1

2 & 3

Directions for use

1. The child places the proper coins in each section.

NUMBER GAME #1

Directions for making game

1 The name of the game is placed on the cover page.

2 A square, 3½″ x 3½″, is drawn on the left center page where playing cards are to be placed.

3 A grid, 7½″ x 10½″, is drawn on the right center page. It is divided into 1½″ squares.

4 Twenty-two playing cards, 3″ x 3½″ are made, each containing one of the following numerals:

0, 0, 1, 1, 1, -1, -1, -1, 2, 2, 2, -2, -2, -2, 3, 3, 3, 4, 4, 4, 4, 5

5 A pocket is constructed on the back cover to hold cards.

6 Directions for play may be typed on paper and glued on the back cover before the game is laminated.

7 Two different colored chips are needed for play.

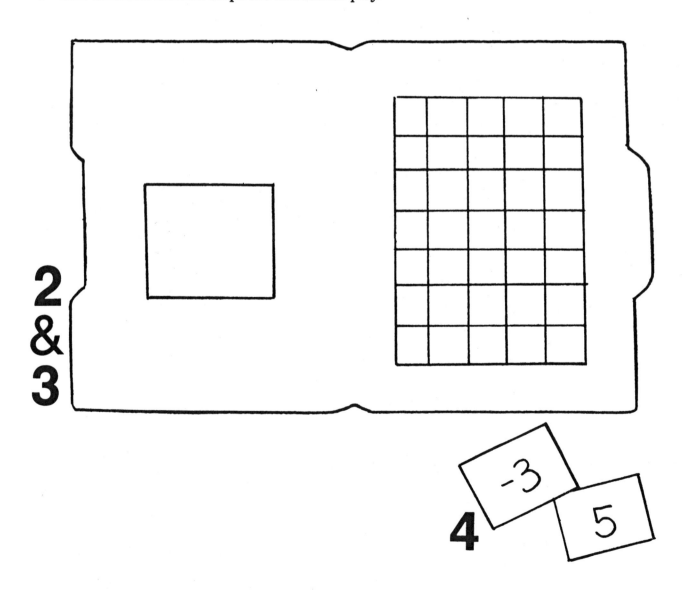

NUMBER GAME #1 continued

Directions for play

1. Each player selects playing chips.

2. The playing cards are placed face-down on the folder.

3. Players take turns drawing a card. They either add or subtract chips to the board as indicated on the card. If they have no chips on the board when a negative number is drawn, they forfeit that turn.

4. After all cards have been drawn, each child counts the number of chips he/she has on the board. The player with the most chips wins.

5. Winners may sign their names to a "winners" sheet.

sign-up sheet

date _____

WINNERS

MEASURE THE PERIMETERS

Directions for making activity

1 The name of the activity is placed on the cover page.

2 Straight-lined drawings are made on the center pages.
Optional: inches or centimeters may be written in.

3 A specially prepared worksheet is provided.

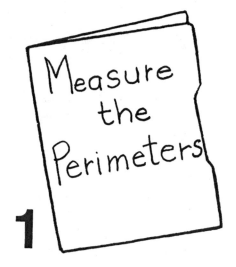

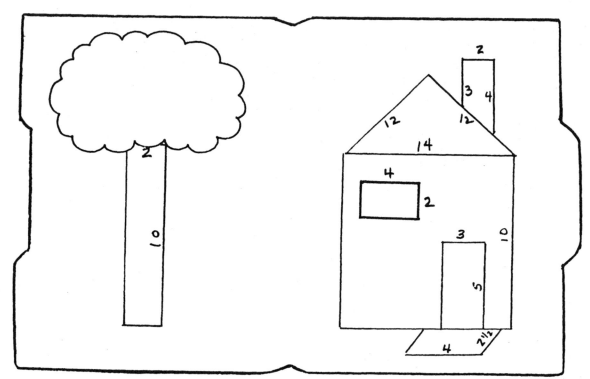

Directions for use

1. The child fills in the answers on the worksheet by adding the given measurements and finding the perimeters.

Note: If measurements are omitted, the child uses a centimeter ruler and measures each line first.

From *Bloomin' Bulletin Boards* by Elaine Commins, Copyright, 1984, Humanics Ltd. P.O. Box 7447, Atlanta, Ga. 30309.

COMPUTER-WISE

Directions for making activity

1 The name of the activity is placed on the cover page along with a cartoon drawing of a computer.

2 A manila envelope to hold computer cards is taped to the left center page.

3 A computer is drawn on the right center page. It is 3″ x 4½″ and contains three rows of various colored self-stick circles—seven pairs and one extra color. (Suggested colors are red, green, blue, orange, yellow, brown, purple. The extra color may be pink.)

4 The file folder is then laminated.

5 Twenty computer cards (3″ x 4½″) are prepared. A math problem, either addition, subtraction, etc. is written on each card. Three holes are punched on each card. Three answers to the problem are written next to each hole. One of the answers is the correct answer. All of the answers on one card are written in one color—which placed over the computer—will show the correct color on the card, thus indicating the correct answer.

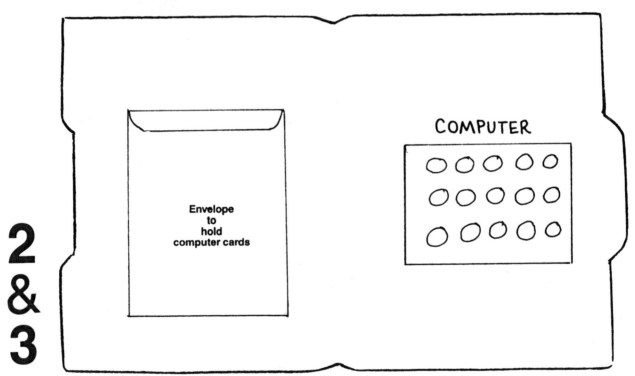

Directions for use

1. The child picks a computer card and either mentally or with paper and pencil decides on the correct answer.

2. To check the answer, the child places the card over the computer on the file folder and if the correct answer has been written in purple, the purple circle will show through the hole.

Computer card

All numbers on this card are written in purple. When placed over the computer, the purple circle will show through the hole marked 18, matching the color on the number and indicating the correct answer.

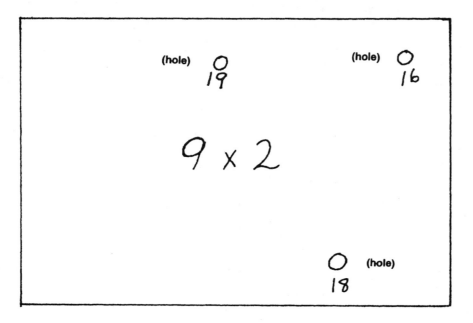

Computer

All circles are self-stick colored circles.

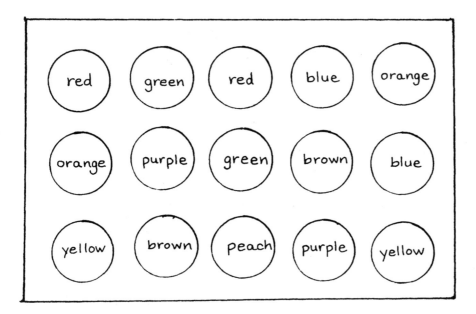

ANSWER THE PHONE

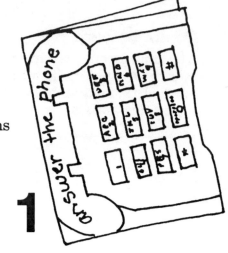

Directions for making activity

1 A telephone is drawn on the cover page. Twelve pushbuttons are drawn with the correct letters and numbers written in.

2 Worksheets are specially prepared for this activity. Worksheets contain a list of words with empty boxes next to them to be filled in with the value of each letter.

3 Worksheets may be stored inside the folder.

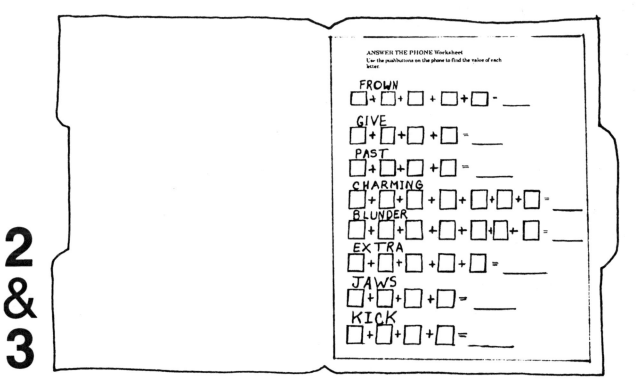

Directions for use

1. Using a worksheet, the child refers to the letters on the push-buttons, finds the value of each letter and records it in the empty box. Adding (or subtracting) all the numbers in the boxes gives the answer.

A sample of a worksheet made for this activity is given on the following page.

ANSWER THE PHONE Worksheet

Use the pushbuttons on the phone to find the value of each letter.

FROWN

□ + □ + □ + □ + □ = _____

GIVE

□ + □ + □ + □ = _____

PAST

□ + □ + □ + □ = _____

CHARMING

□ + □ + □ + □ + □ + □ + □ = _____

BLUNDER

□ + □ + □ + □ + □ + □ + □ = _____

EXTRA

□ + □ + □ + □ + □ = _____

JAWS

□ + □ + □ + □ = _____

KICK

□ + □ + □ + □ = _____

120

BRAINY BALLOONS

Directions for making activity

1 The name of the activity is placed on the cover page.

2 The center pages are filled with drawings of balloons. Various colors such as green, red, yellow, blue and purple are used.

3 Addition and subtraction problems relating to the balloons are printed on the back cover page.

4 Pencils and paper are provided.

1

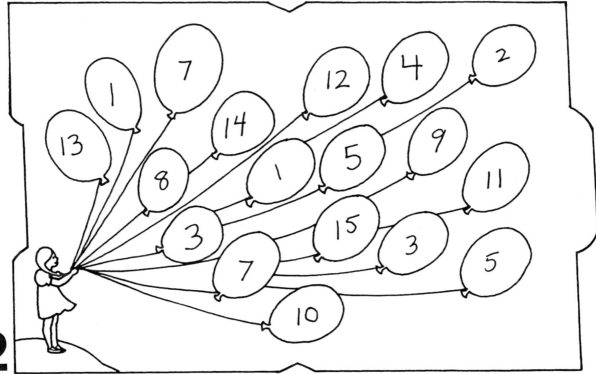

2

Directions for use

1. Add all the numbers in the red balloons. (Then, green, blue, etc.)

2. How many balloons are there?

3. What is the sum of all the balloons?

4. Subtract the number of blue balloons from the red balloons.

5. Add the green and purple balloons, then subtract the orange balloons.

6. How many balloons are there with numbers written on them that are ten or less?

7. How many even numbered balloons are there? Odd?

8. What is the lowest number on the balloons? The highest? Counting from the lowest to the highest, which numbers are missing on the balloons?

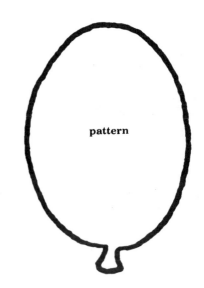

pattern

MAY THE FOURS BE WITH YOU

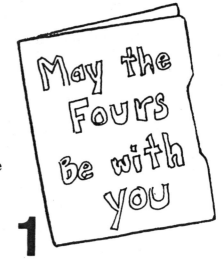

Directions for making activity

1 The name of the activity is placed on the cover page.

2 Directions are printed on the left center page.

3 Worksheets containing a line for each child in the class are prepared by the teacher. Worksheets may conveniently be stapled to the right center page for keeping.

4 Differing amounts of chips are drawn next to each child's name on the worksheet.

2 & 3 & 4

Directions

A box of chips falls to the floor in the classroom and chips spill all over.

The names of all your classmates are given on the worksheet with the number of chips each one finds.

Remember, each chip shown equals four.

Write the answers in the proper column of each line.

names	chips	ans.
Lisa	OOO	
Sam	OOOOOOO	
Joyce	OOOOO	
Gerald	OOOOOO	
Laney	OOOO	
Jeff	OOOO	
Jodi	OOOOOOO	
Cayla	OOOOOO	
Julie	OOOOOOOO	
Gary	OOOOOO	
Marty	OOOOO	
Carole	OOOO	
Billy	OOOOOO	
Cathy	OOO	
Ricky	OO	
Kate	O	
Jeremy	OOOO	

Directions for use

1. The child removes a worksheet from the folder.

2. Each chip on the worksheet represents four chips.

3. The chips are counted and answers are written in each space.

Suggestion: Counting by threes, fives, sixes, etc. may also be incorporated in this kind of worksheet. Other symbols such as footballs, phonograph records, etc. may be used instead of chips.

MULTIPLICATION EXERCISE

Directions for making exercise

1 The name of the exercise is placed on the cover page.

2 A pocket is constructed on the left center page to hold cards.

3 A grid is constructed on the right center page. Numbers from 1-9 are written across the top of the grid and down the left side.

4 Small square cards, sized to fit into the squares on the grid are prepared. Each card contains the product of the multiplication facts.

2 & 3

envelope to hold cards

pocket to hold cards

1	2	3	4	5	6	7	8	9
2	·	·	·	·	·	·	·	·
3	·	·	12	·	·	·	·	·
4	·	·	·	·	·	·	·	·
5	·	·	·	·	·	·	·	·
6	·	·	·	·	36	·	·	·
7	·	·	·	·	·	·	·	·
8	·	·	·	·	·	·	·	·
9	·	·	·	·	·	·	·	·

Directions for use

1. The child looks down and across a column to find the multiplication facts, then selecting the correct answer on one of the cards, places it in the proper square.

Suggestion: Two or three identical playing boards may be offered children at the same time so that several students can work the exercise together.

4

MULTIPLICATION 36

Directions for making activity

1. The name of the activity is placed on the cover page.

2. A grid, 7″ x 8½″, is drawn on the right center page. Combinations of two or three numbers that equal 36 when multiplied together–either up, down or diagonally–are written in the grid randomly. Remaining spaces are filled with numbers less than 36.

3. A specially prepared worksheet is provided.

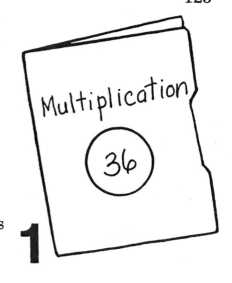

1

2

18	10	11	9	2	2	4	8
6	2	4	7	3	14	15	3
9	3	1	4	6	21	19	11
13	2	3	7	1	5	16	12
4	0	2	21	17	18	20	5
7	5	3	6	7	2	18	8
2	3	6	4	12	3	9	11
3	13	22	16	4	19	4	20
4	2	10	9	36	7	4	20
8	1	6	5	1	2	6	8

Directions for use

1. Children must copy all of the numbers found on the file folder grid onto their worksheet grid.

2. They draw a closed line around any two or three numbers (horizontally, vertically or diagonally) which, when multiplied together, equal 36.

Suggestion: Other combinations of numbers may be used.

Pattern for MULTIPLICATION 36

FRACTION GAME

Directions for making game

1 The name of the game is placed on the cover page.

2 A grid with 20 squares is drawn on the right center page. In each section of the grid, a geometric shape is drawn with clearly identifiable areas. Parts of the areas are shaded in.

3 Two or three sets of 20 fraction cards which correspond to the fractions on the shapes are constructed. (Index cards are suitable for this purpose.) In addition, three blank cards are inserted in the deck.

The following fractions are written on the cards: $\frac{1}{4}$, $\frac{1}{3}$, $\frac{1}{2}$, $\frac{2}{3}$, $\frac{3}{4}$, $\frac{1}{5}$, $\frac{2}{5}$, $\frac{3}{5}$, $\frac{4}{5}$, $\frac{1}{6}$, $\frac{5}{6}$, $\frac{1}{7}$, $\frac{2}{7}$, $\frac{3}{7}$, $\frac{4}{7}$, $\frac{1}{8}$, $\frac{3}{8}$, $\frac{7}{8}$, and 1.

4 A file folder is provided for each player.

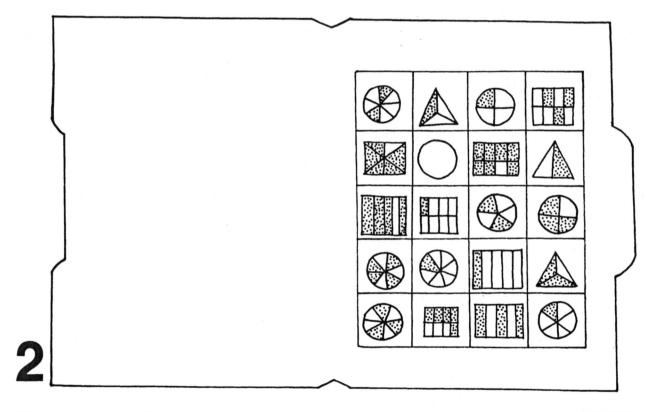

Directions for play

1. Cards are placed face-down on the table.

2. Players take turns drawing a card. If the fraction on the card corresponds with one of the shaded shapes on the grid, the card is placed over the shape. If the card does not match, it is returned to the bottom of the deck.

3. The first player to cover his/her entire grid wins.

4. If a blank card is drawn, the player loses a turn.

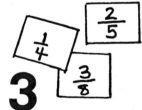

Pattern for FRACTION GAME

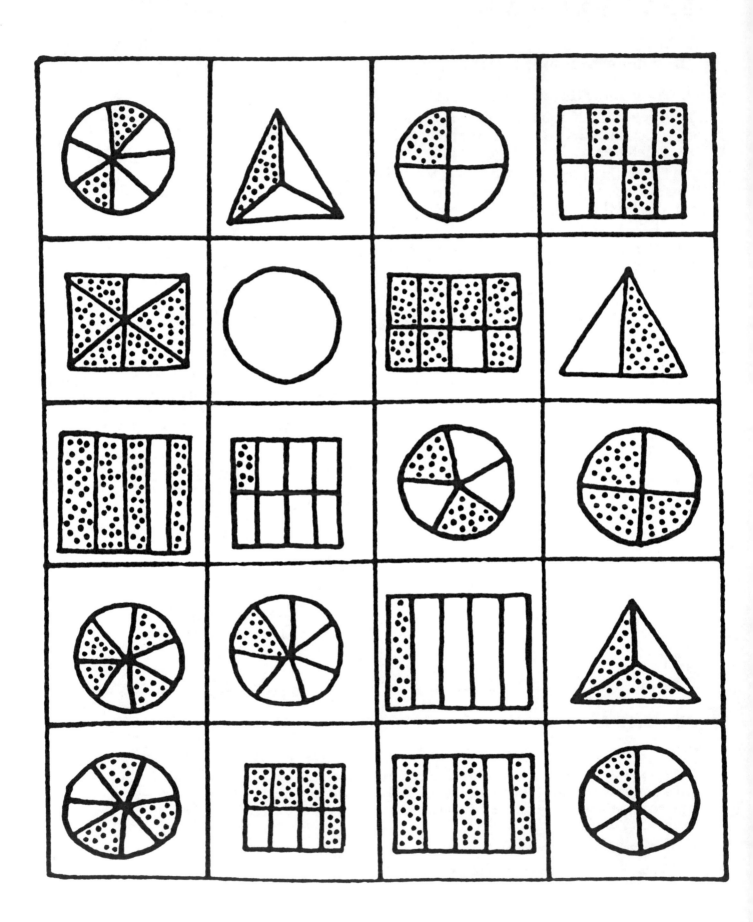

ANSWERS ON CLOTHESPINS

Directions for making activity

1. The name of the activity is placed on the cover page.

2. Sections are drawn around the border of the center page. In each section a multiplication problem is posed.

3. Clothespins with the answers to the problems written on them with permanent markers are provided.

4. The file folder is then laminated.

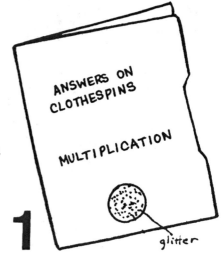

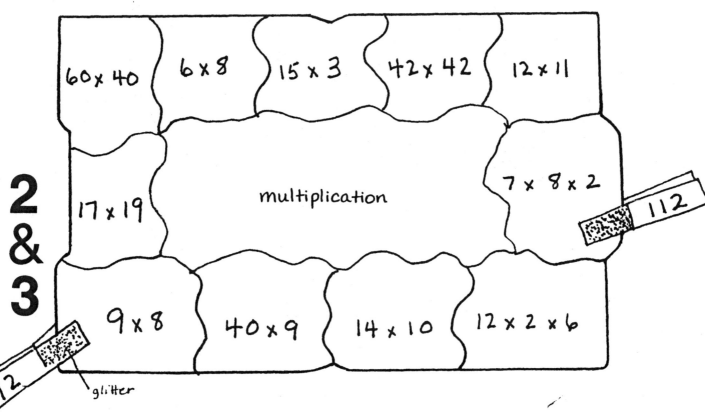

Directions for use

1. The student clips the clothespins to the matching problems in each section.

Suggestion: *Color coding several file folders with similar activities that include subtraction, division, fractions and word problems is suggested.*

MONKEY MATH

Directions for making activity

1 The name of the activity is placed on the cover page.

2 Directions are printed on the left center page.

3 Worksheets with rhyming word problems are stapled to the right center page.

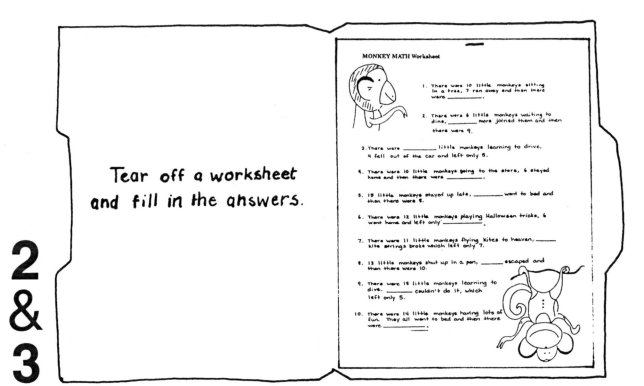

Directions for use

1. The child detaches a worksheet and fills in the answers.

An example of a worksheet is given on the following page.

MONKEY MATH Worksheet

1. There were 10 little monkeys sitting in a tree, 7 ran away and then there were _____.

2. There were 6 little monkeys waiting to dine, _____ more joined them and then there were 9.

3. There were _____ little monkeys learning to drive, 4 fell out of the car and left only 5.

4. There were 10 little monkeys going to the store, 6 stayed home and then there were _____.

5. 15 little monkeys stayed up late, _____ went to bed and then there were 8.

6. There were 12 little monkeys playing Halloween tricks, 6 went home and left only _____.

7. There were 11 little monkeys flying kites to heaven, _____ kite strings broke which left only 7.

8. 13 little monkeys shut up in a pen, _____ escaped and then there were 10.

9. There were 18 little monkeys learning to dive. _____ couldn't do it, which left only 5.

10. There were 14 little monkeys having lots of fun. They all went to bed and then there were _____.

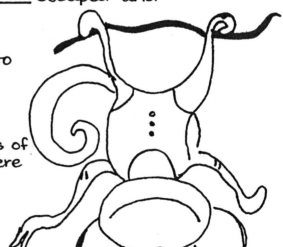

Chapter 5

Science

The folder games in this chapter focus on high-interest projects for the six, seven, and eight-year-old student. Some of the subjects included are: animals, maps, and the planets and stars.

ANIMALS-Where They Live

Directions for making activity

1 The name of the activity is placed on the cover page.

2 Six pockets are glued to the center pages. Each pocket is labelled with the habitat of various animals. Pictures and/or drawings may be used also.

3 Numerous cards are prepared. Each contains a picture of an animal. The cards may be kept in a plastic ziplock bag or a box.

4 The file folder is then laminated.

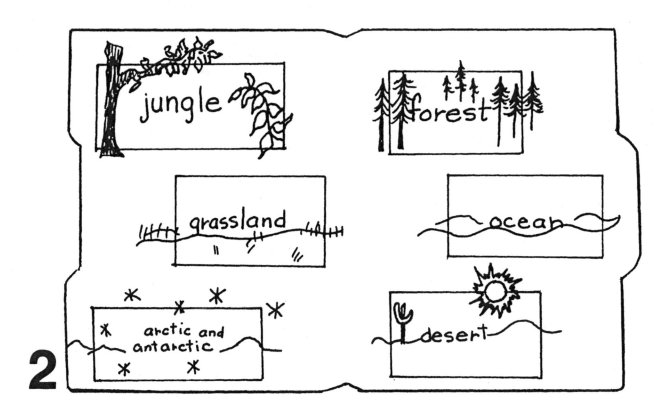

Directions for use

1. The child places each animal card in the proper pocket on the folder.

ANIMALS–What They Eat

Directions for making activity

1 The name of the activity is placed on the cover page.

2 Three pockets are constructed on the center pages. They are labelled either herbivorous, carnivorous or omnivorous.

3 A series of animal-picture cards is prepared.

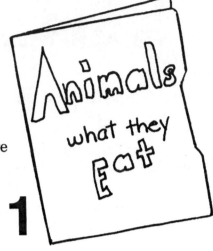

1

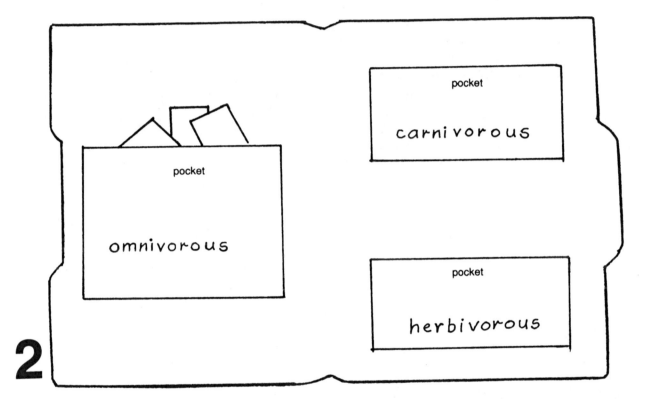

2

Directions for use

1. The child categorizes the animals into herbivorous, carnivorous or omnivorous and places them in the proper pocket on the folder.

3

THE BUTTERFLY- Sequencing Life Cycles

Directions for making activity

1 The name of the activity is placed on the cover.

2 Numbered squares from one to six are drawn on the center pages.

3 A set of six drawings of the life cycle of a butterfly is duplicated, cut out, glued to oak tag, and then laminated.

4 A pocket is constructed on the back cover to hold the six drawings.

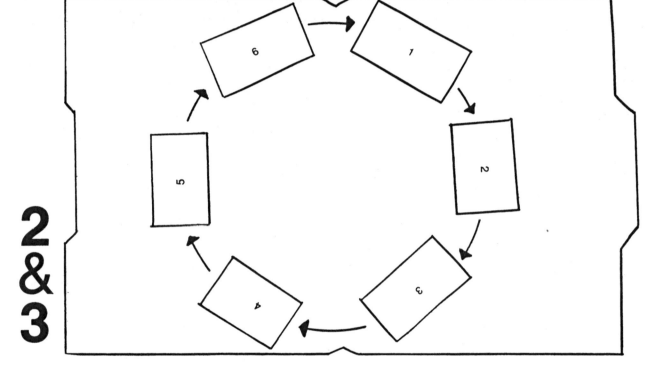

Directions for use

1. Students arrange the drawings in sequence on the center pages.

Note: Patterns for a butterfly plus patterns for the life cycle of a frog are given on the following pages.

Patterns for THE FROG

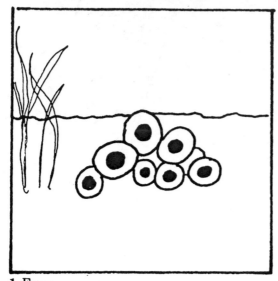

1. Eggs

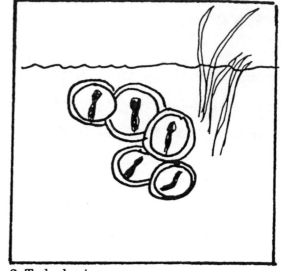

2. Tadpoles in eggs

3. Newly born tadpole

4. Tadpole with hind legs

5. Tadpole with forelegs

6. Adult frog

Patterns for THE BUTTERFLY

1. Eggs

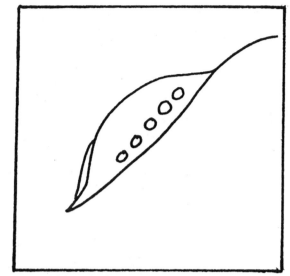

2. Larvae forming in the eggs

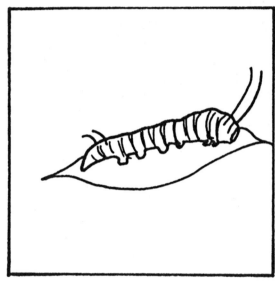

3. Caterpillar

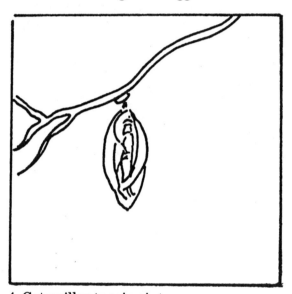

4. Caterpillar turning into a pupa

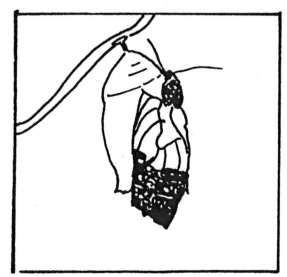

5. Butterfly emerging from the pupa

6. Adult Monarch butterfly

VITAMINS

Directions for making activity

1. The name of the activity is placed on the cover page.

2. Using magazines and seed catalogues, pictures of food are cut out and pasted on the center pages. Each food should be rich in one or more vitamins. Sources include:

Vitamin A–milk, eggs, liver, green and yellow vegetables, sweet potatoes, etc.

Vitamin B–fish, poultry, porkchops, cereal, peanut butter, whole grain bread, etc.

Vitamin C–tomatoes, oranges, grapefruit, strawberries, potatoes, lemons, etc.

Vitamin D–egg yolks, milk, tunafish, etc.

3. A prepared worksheet is provided. It should contain four columns, each headed by one of the vitamins.

Directions for use

1. The child sorts the pictured foods according to their primary vitamin content and lists them in the proper column on the worksheet.

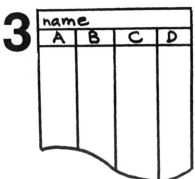

MIXING COLORS

Directions for making activity

1 The name of the activity is placed on the cover page.

2 From six to ten numbered lines are drawn on the center pages.

3 On each of the lines, colored gummed circles are used as part of a quiz. For example: blue (circle) + red (circle) = ?

4 A specially prepared worksheet with blank circles is provided along with plastic cups for mixing paint and paintbrushes.

5 Primary and/or secondary colors may be used. One jar of paint for each color is placed on the table.

Directions for use

1. The student paints the first two blank circles on each line of the worksheet to match those given on the folder. He/she then mixes the two colors together to discover the color for the last circle on the line and paints it in.

2. Each student washes brushes and cups after use.

PLACING THE PLANETS[3]

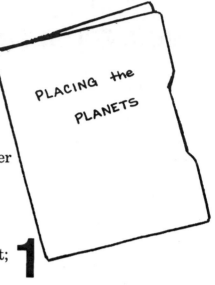

Directions for making activity

1 The name of the activity is placed on the cover page.

2 The edge of the sun (very large) is drawn on the left center page. Nine paths (orbits) are drawn next to the sun on the center pages.

3 A pocket is constructed on the back page to hold planets.

4 Nine planets are drawn and cut out of poster board. Their names are written on each. A fact about each planet may be written on the reverse side. For example: It is the hottest planet; it is the largest planet; it was the last planet to be discovered.

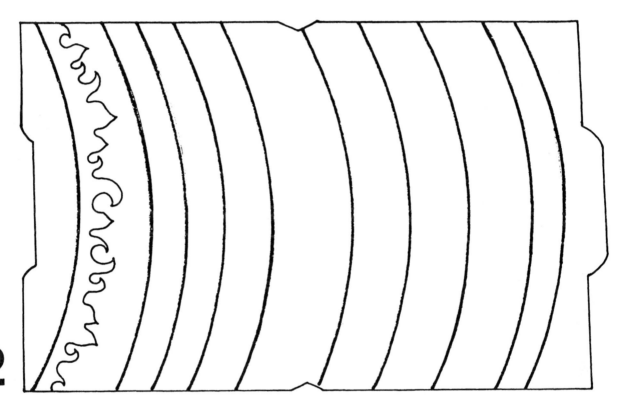

Directions for use

1. The child places the planets on their orbits in order of their proximity to the sun.

Suggestion: *The sentence– "My Very Educated Mother Just Served Us Nine Pizzas" is a helpful learning tool. The first letter of each word is the same as the first letter in each of the planets. Mercury, Venus, Earth, Mars, Jupiter, Saturn, Uranus, Neptune and Pluto are the planets in order of their proximity to the sun.*

3. This idea from *Early Childhood Activities* by Elaine Commins, copyright 1982 by Humanics Limited, P.O. Box 7447, Atlanta, Georgia 30309, pgs. 227-228

CONSTELLATIONS

Directions for making activity

1 The name of the activity and the particular constellation are placed on the cover page.

2 A constellation is drawn on the right center page. Gummed silver stars and glitter may be used to decorate.

3 The folder is then laminated.

4 Colored construction paper, crayons, glitter, gummed stars, yarn, marking pens, etc. are provided.

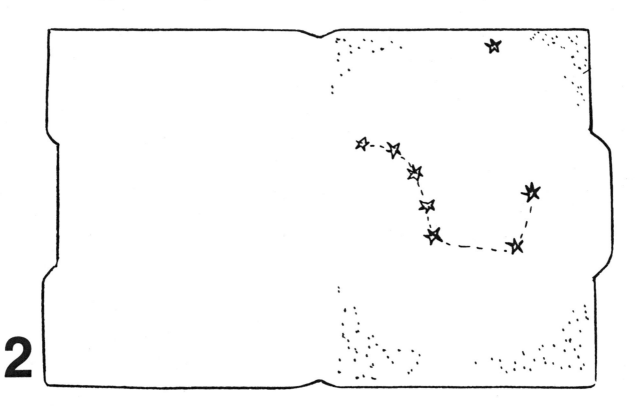

Directions for use

1. The child draws and labels the constellation on his/her paper.
2. Several folders, each containing a different constellation are prepared to be offered at the same time.

Suggestion: After completing four or five constellation papers, the teacher may staple the child's work together to make a constellation booklet.

Drawings of several constellations are given on the following page.

Patterns for CONSTELLATIONS

FLOW CHARTS

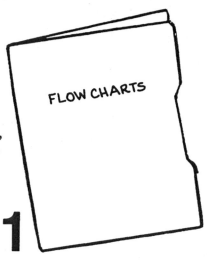

Directions for making activity

Patterned after an exercise used in the British Infant Schools, this activity allows the students to design various ways of investigating a single topic.

1 The name of the activity is placed on the cover page.

2 An example of a Flow Chart is typed and pasted on the left center page.

3 Topics for the child to prepare in making his/her own Flow Chart are given on the right center page.

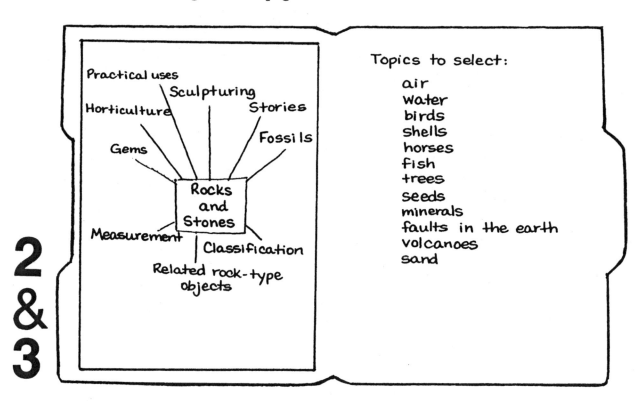

Directions for use

1. A student discussion is held as a preliminary exercise before work is begun.

2. The student uses the example as a model and designs his/her own Flow Chart.

An example of a Flow Chart is given on the following page.

FLOW CHART–Study of rocks

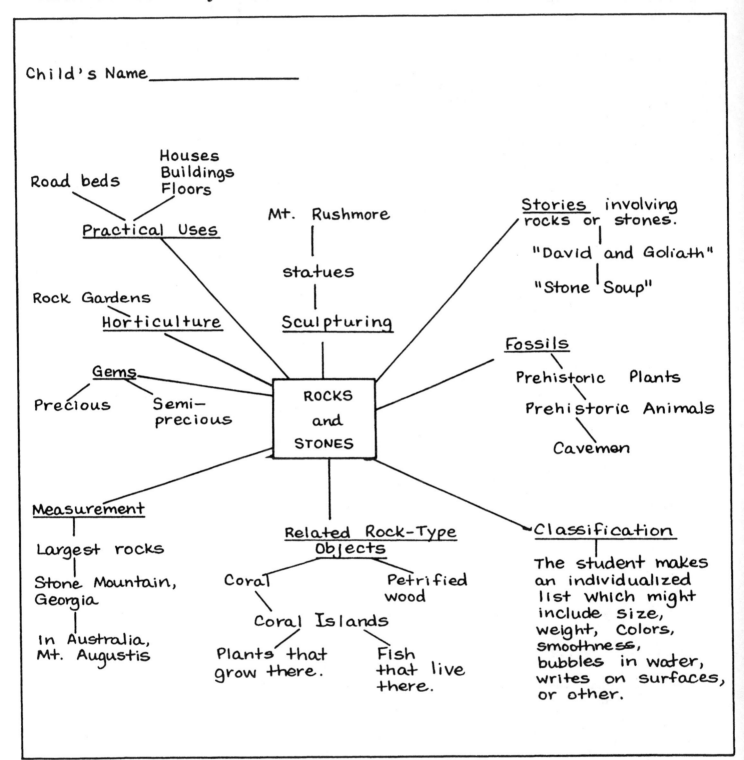

A Flow Chart can be applied to social studies as well as science. Topics such as favorite books, favorite illustrators, fairy tales from many countries, folk tales, a particular century, religious holidays around the world, all about the Beatles, movies about space, etc. may be used.

MAP TRACING

Directions for making activity

1 The name of the activity is placed on the cover page.

2 On the right center page, the outline of a country is drawn using a black, water-color, felt-tipped marker. The map's interior may be colored with a lighter color such as yellow.

3 Tracing paper, felt-tipped pens and crayons are provided.

4 The file folder should be laminated.

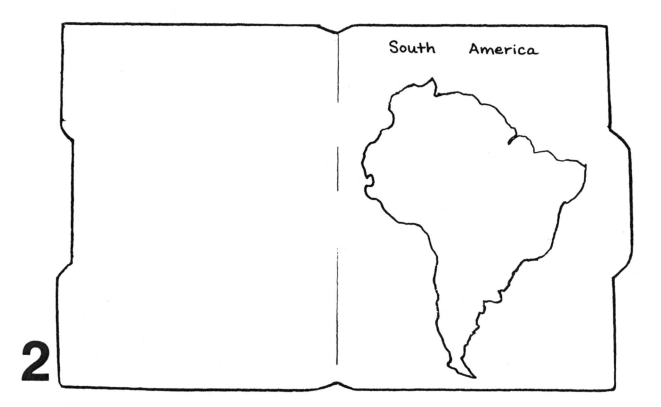

Directions for use

1. The child places the tracing paper over the map and traces it.

Suggestion: *Several tracings of continents may be made by students, then stapled together to form a booklet.*
Patterns for the six continents are given on the following pages.

Pattern for South America

Pattern for North America

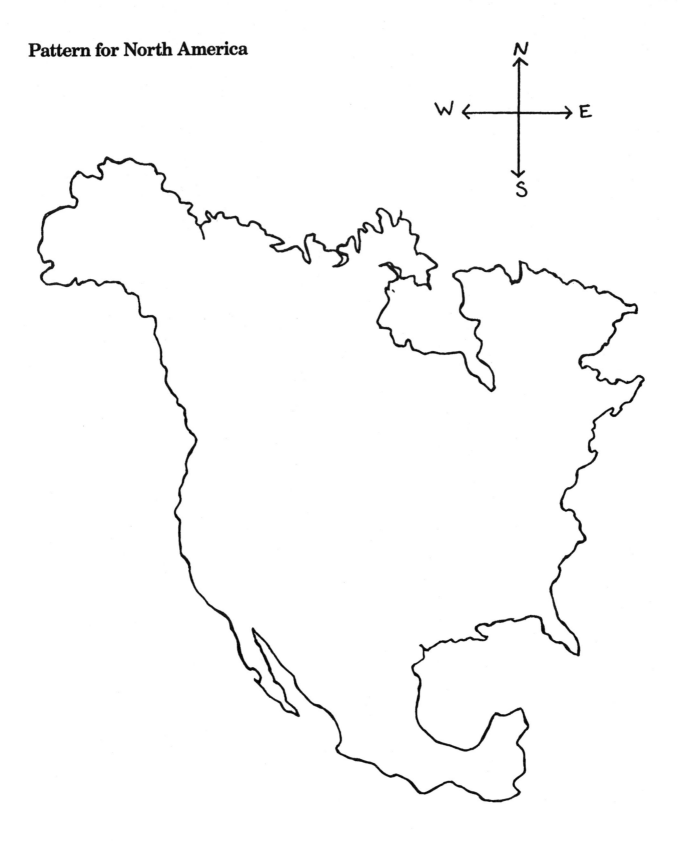

Pattern for Europe

Pattern for Asia

Pattern for Africa

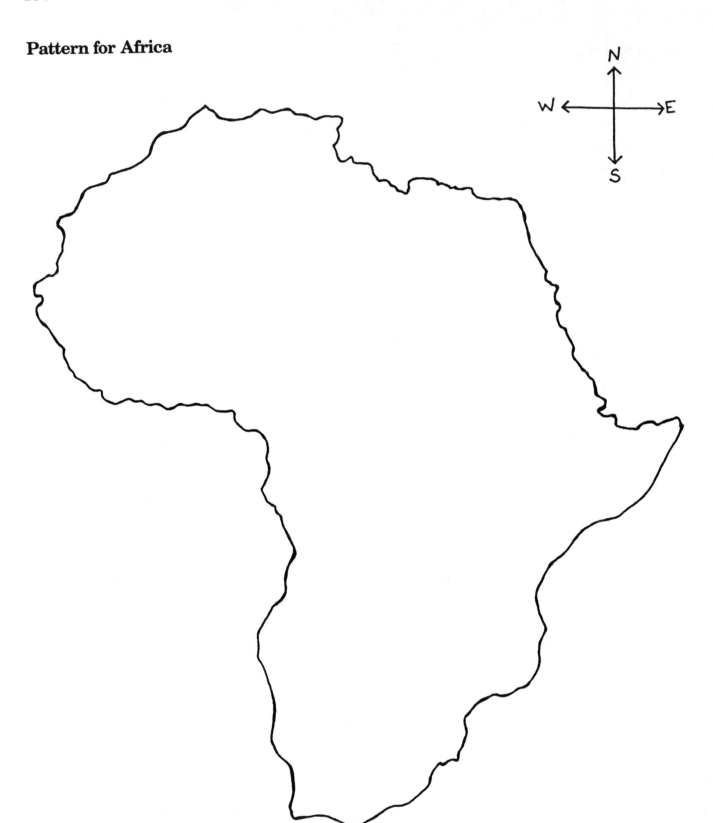

Pattern for Australia

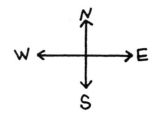

ANIMAL CATEGORIES

Directions for making activity

1 The name of the activity is placed on the cover page.

2 Small pictures of animals are pasted entirely over the inner pages. A variety of animal categories such as mammals, fish, birds, amphibians, insects and reptiles should be included.

3 A worksheet listing the various categories should be offered.

Directions for use

1. The student writes the name of each animal category in its proper place on the worksheet.

■ A sample worksheet is given on the following page.

ANIMAL CATEGORIES WORKSHEET

amphibians

reptiles

insects

fish

birds

mammals

MAGNETS

Directions for making activity

1 The name of the activity is placed on the cover page.

2 The left inner page of the file folder is labelled "magnetic." The right inner page is labelled "non-magnetic."

3 A magnet and a shoe box filled with items such as chalk, a penny, a gem clip, pencil, staple, nail file, scissors, piece of cloth, marble, rubber band, eraser, bottlecap, nail, string, eraser, key, safety pin, etc. are provided.

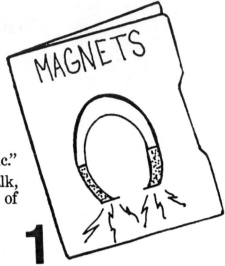

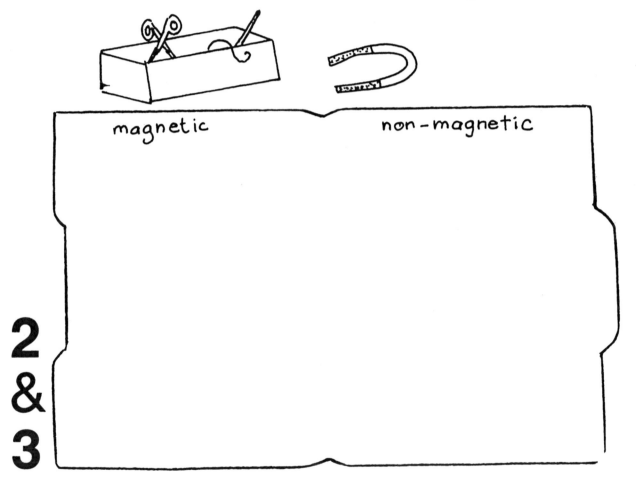

magnetic   non-magnetic

Directions for use

1. Using the magnet the student tests each item and places it on the proper page.

2. To further enhance the lesson, the student might be asked to list all the magnetic items on a paper.

HOW ANIMALS MOVE

Directions for making activity

1 The name of the activity is placed on the cover page.

2 Six vertical columns are drawn on the center pages. The following labels are printed at the top of each column: walk, run, crawl, swim, jump and fly.

3 Many pictures of animals are mounted on oak tag and placed in a plastic "baggie" to accompany this folder.

1

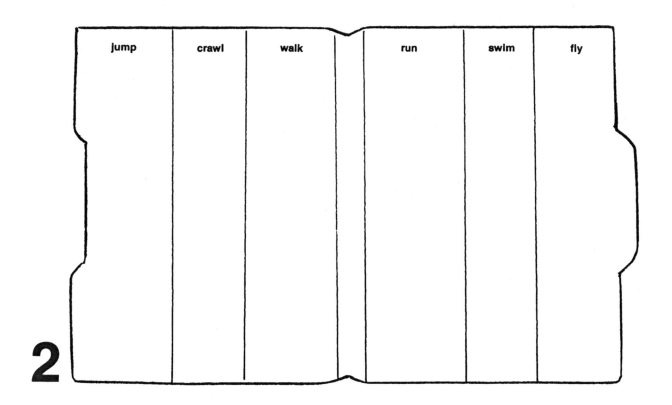

jump	crawl	walk	run	swim	fly

2

Directions for use

1. The student places the animal pictures in the proper column.

■ Suggestion: Animal pictures are often found in old workbooks.

DINOSAUR MURAL

Directions for making activity

1 The name of the activity is placed on the cover page.

2 A large pocket is constructed on each of the inner pages to hold dinosaur patterns. Patterns should be made out of cardboard.

3 Pencils, scissors and colored construction paper are provided.

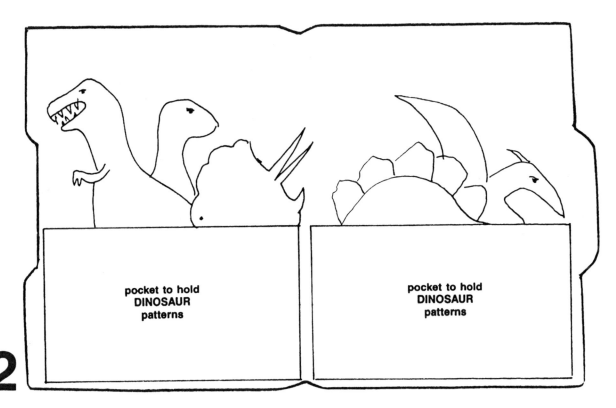

Directions for use

1. A long piece of kraft paper or wrapping paper is tacked on the bulletin board. It may be decorated with a hilly landscape or mountains, etc.

2. As many as five or six students at a time may trace and cut out dinosaurs and tape them on the mural. Names of dinosaurs should be printed on each cut-out.

■ Dinosaur patterns are given on the following pages.

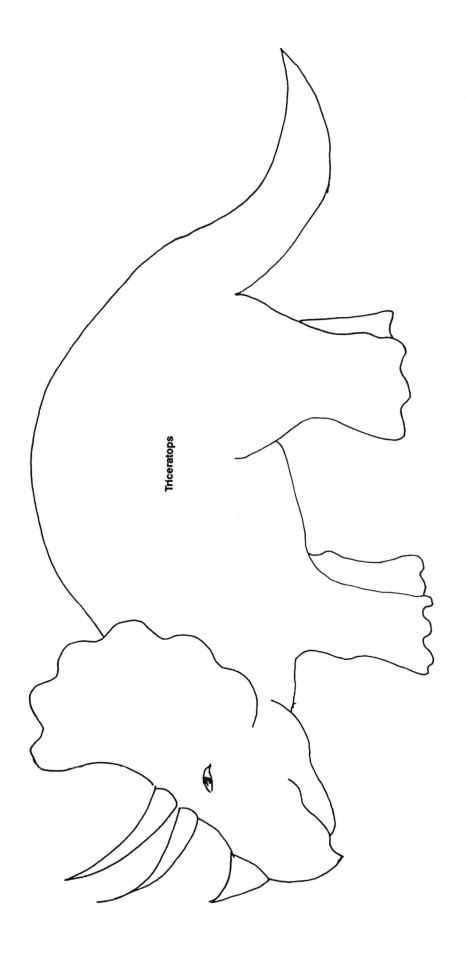

Triceratops

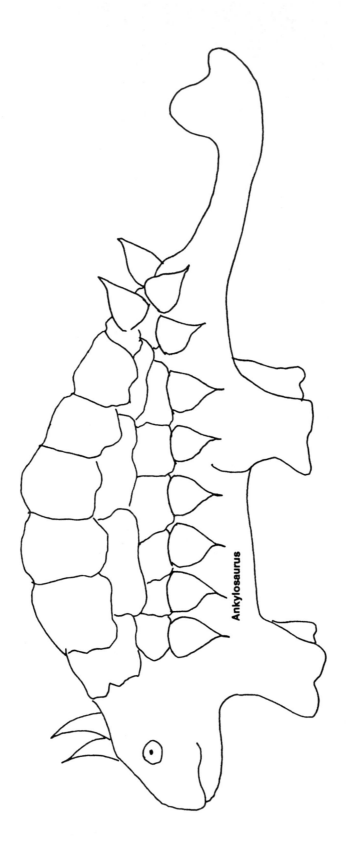

Ankylosaurus

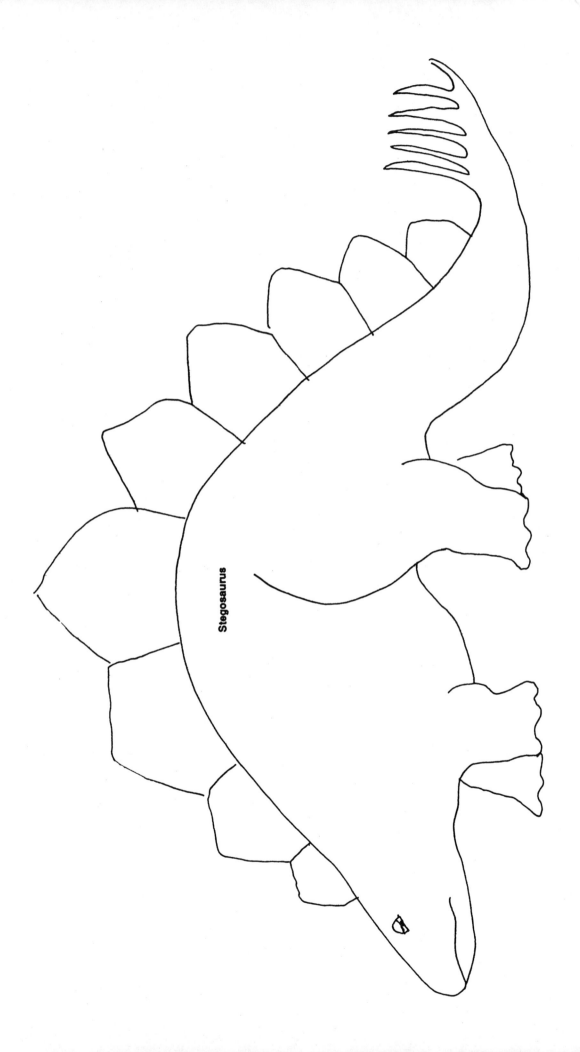

Stegosaurus

Brontosaurus

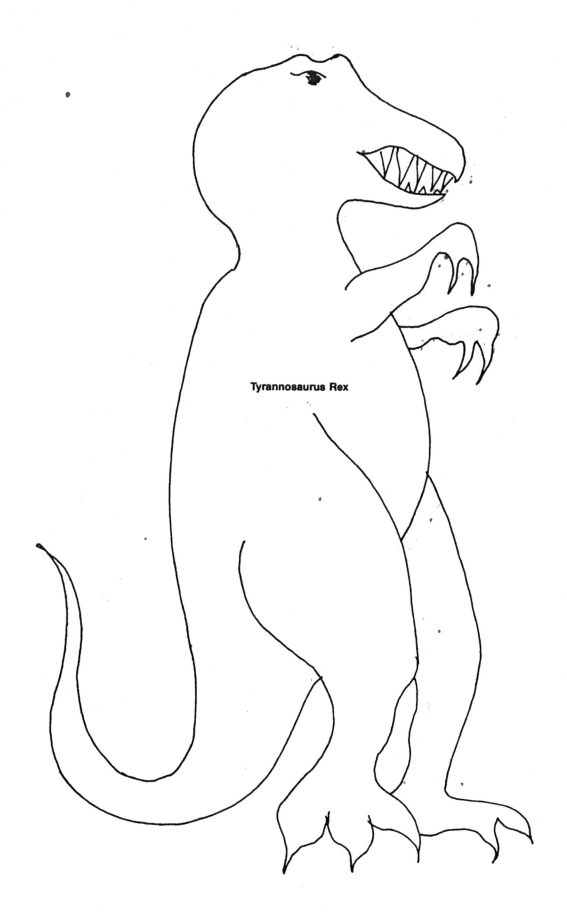

Tyrannosaurus Rex

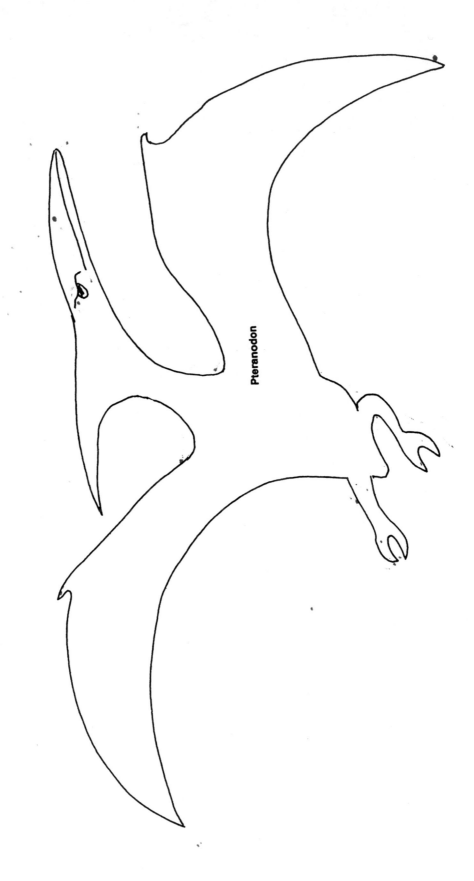

Pteranodon

PRODUCTS FROM PLANTS

Directions for making activity

1 The name of the activity is placed on the cover page.

2 Five vertical columns are drawn on the center pages.

3 Many pictures of plants such as trees, bushes, flowers, shrubs, vegetables, cotton plants, etc. are mounted on oak tag and placed in a plastic "baggie" to accompany this folder.

4 The five vertical columns are labelled: FOOD, CLOTHING, BEAUTY, BUILDINGS, WOOD PRODUCTS.

FOOD	CLOTHING	BUILDINGS	BEAUTY	WOOD PRODUCTS

Directions for use

1. The student places the plant pictures in the proper column.

■ Suggestion: Plant pictures can be obtained from old workbooks, magazines and old textbooks.

Chapter 6

Social Studies

Subjects included in social studies programs are usually diverse. Each of the folder games exercises that are included here are geared to stimulate thinking skills through quizzes, discussions, and essays.

Topics presented in this text are related to self concepts, economics, occupations, government, and sports.

CHRISTOPHER COLUMBUS

Directions for making game

1. The name of the game is placed on the cover page along with decorations.

2. A grid is drawn on the center pages. A ship is drawn on the center spaces to indicate the starting point of the game.

3. A drawing of 8 points of the compass is made next to the grid.

4. 16 playing cards are made instructing players to move either 1 or 2 spaces toward a point on the compass. For example:

"Go N 1 space"

"Go SE 2 spaces"

5. Markers representing the Nina, the Pinta and the Santa Maria are provided.

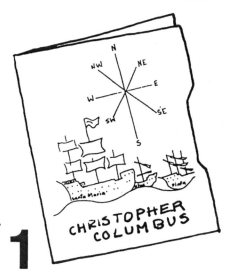

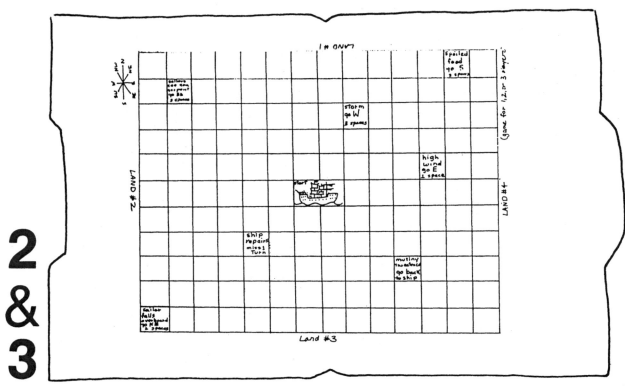

Directions for play

1. The player draws a card and, starting on the center ship, moves in the direction stated.

2. Players must touch all 4 land areas to win. After each landing, markers are returned to the ship.

3. If a player cannot move in the direction stated, another card is drawn.

An example of a game board is given on the following page.

Grid for CHRISTOPHER COLUMBUS

SW W NW
S · N
SE E NE

sailor falls overboard go NE 2 spaces

sailors see sea serpent go SE 3 spaces

ship repairs miss 1 turn

start

storm go W 3 spaces

Land #3

LAND #1

mutiny threatened go back to ship

high wind go E 1 space

spoiled food go S 2 spaces

LAND #4

(game for 1, 2, or 3 players)

NAME THE CITIES

Directions for making activity

1 The name of the activity is placed on the cover page along with the map to be used.

2 Principal cities are pin-pointed and lines are drawn from them to rectangular lift-panels. The lift-panels are cut out on three sides.

3 Answers are located directly behind the lift-panels–on the right center page of the folder.

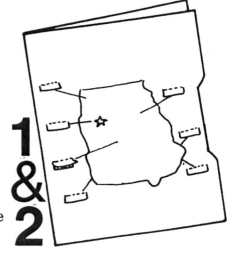

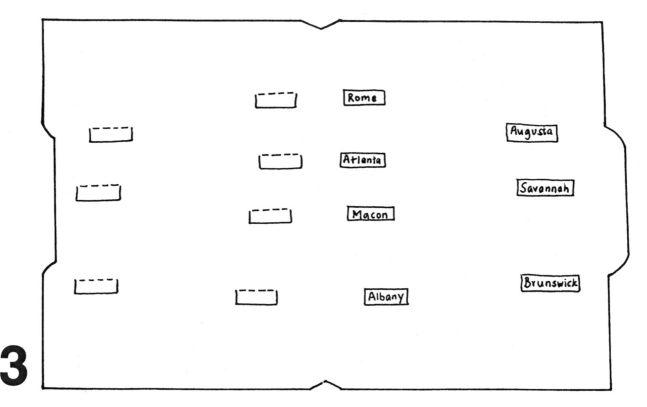

Directions for use

1. The child identifies each city by location and lifts the answer panel to check for correctness.

2. Children may check each other's answers and a sign-up sheet may be used.

Suggestion: *Several maps of this kind may be offered at the same time. Each would focus in on a different topic such as rivers, mountains, products, etc.*

In addition, when displaying maps of continents, students could identify countries, capitals, etc.

DIRECTIONS

Directions for making activity

1 The name of the activity is placed on the cover page.

2 A sample map–either a map from school to the teacher's house or a fictitious map–is drawn on the left center page.

3 Instructions on using the map are given on the right center page.

4 The file folder is then laminated.

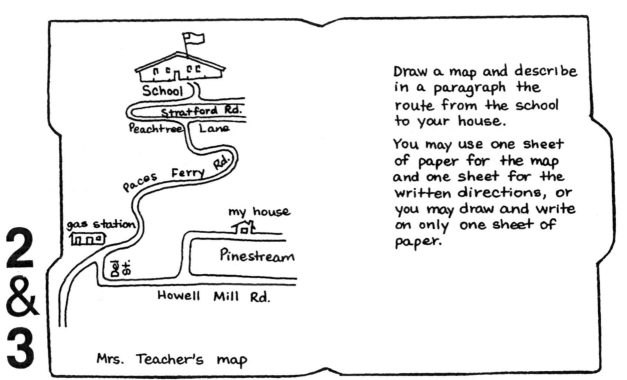

Directions for use

1. The child observes the sample map. He/she then draws a map describing the route from his/her home to the school.

Suggestions: *Other maps that may be used for this activity include a map of the school, a map of the schoolroom, a map of the child's home, the route from school to a park, shopping center or other.*

DON'T OPEN

Directions for making activity

1 The directions are placed on the cover page along with "DON'T OPEN."

2 An action picture, preferably one depicting some human emotion, is cut out of a magazine and pasted on the right center page.

3 A small area is cut around the main character's face on the cover page.

4 The file folder is then laminated.

Directions for use

1. The child is asked to describe the emotion on the face of the person without opening the folder to find out what that person is actually doing.

Suggestion: A series of folders showing emotions may be offered at the same time. Children are given the opportunity to select one and write about it.

STATE THE FACTS

Directions for making activity

1 The name of the activity is placed on the cover page.
2 A map of the United States is drawn on the center pages.
3 A list of approximately ten questions is written on the back cover.
4 The file folder is then laminated.
5 Paper and pencils are provided.

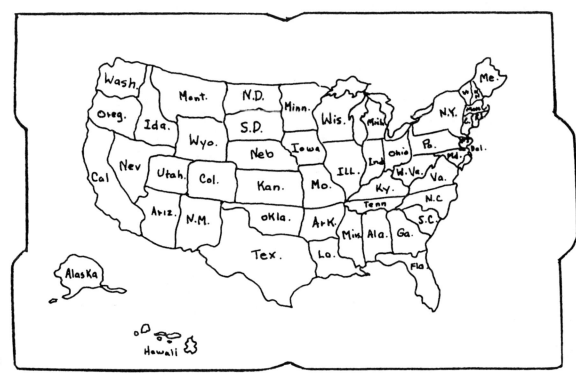

Directions for use

1. Using paper and pencil, the students write the answers to the questions posed on the back cover.

2. Several folders, each asking different questions may be offered at the same time.

A list of the kinds of questions that may be asked is given on the following page.

Questions for STATE THE FACTS:

1. Name the state in which you live.
2. Is it north, south, east or west?
3. List the states that touch your state.
4. Name the state in which you were born.
5. List the states that touch the state in which you were born.
6. In what state is Washington, D.C.?
7. In what state is Mt. Rushmore?
8. In what state is Yellowstone Park?
9. In what state(s) is the San Andreas Fault?
10. What is your state's slogan?
11. What states touch the Mississippi River?
12. In what state is Stone Mountain?
13. What is the most northern state in the U.S.?
14. What state would you like to visit? Why?
15. How many states have two words in their names?
16. Name the states that touch the great lakes.
17. Name the states that touch the Gulf of Mexico.

TAKE A POLL

Directions for making activity

1 The name of the activity is placed on the cover page.
2 Suggestions for topics to be polled are given on the center pages.

Select one of the following topics and list the opinions of your fellow students.

1. Name your 3 favorite TV shows.
2. Name your 3 favorite movies.
3. Name all of the places you have lived.
4. Give me the menu for your favorite meal.
5. If you could travel anywhere, name your first two choices.
6. List the country your parents or grandparents came from before they lived in the United States.
7. If you could buy a new car, which one would it be?
8. What occupation would you like to have when you are grown?
9. What is your favorite sport?
10. At what age do you think people should be allowed to drive a car?
11. How many hours a day do you watch TV?
12. What is your favorite subject in school?
13. Should there be a dress code for students?
14. Should students have their own bank accounts?

Directions for use

1. Each child selects a topic and canvasses students and/or teachers. The recorded results may be posted on a bulletin board.

WRITE AN ESSAY

Directions for making activity

1 The name of the activity is placed on the cover page.
2 Suggestions for topics for essays are given on the center pages.

1

2

Select one of the following topics and write a short essay about it.

1. What is the very first thing in your life that you can remember?
2. What do you think "democracy" means?
3. Why is it important to vote?
4. How should you act if your team loses?
5. What can be done to protect wild animals?
6. Write about your hero.
7. If you inherited a lot of money, would you give some of it to a charity? What charity? Why?
8. What does the word "friendship" mean to you?
9. Do you believe some books should be banned? Why?
10. Do you believe some TV programs should be banned? Why?
11. Name some traits that you think all the people in the world have in common.

Directions for use

1. Each child selects a topic and writes a short essay. Completed work may be posted on the bulletin board or read before the class.

PROBLEMS

Directions for making activity

1 The name of the activity is placed on the cover page.
2 A list of problems of interest to students is printed on the center pages.

1

2

PROBLEMS

1. I feel ugly.
2. I have no friends.
3. Others always tease me.
4. I have bad dreams.
5. The teacher hates me.
6. I hate the teacher.
7. I hate the school lunches.
8. Someone always steals my lunch money.
9. I'm always hungry.
10. I'm too short (tall).
11. We don't own a TV.

PROBLEMS

12. I'm too shy to answer in class.
13. People whisper about me.
14. I lost my library book.
15. I wear ugly clothes.
16. I'm afraid of dogs.
17. Another student keeps hitting me when the teacher isn't looking.
18. I get too sleepy to listen to the teacher.
19. Sometimes I forget to do my homework.

Directions for use

1. The student selects one of the problems and writes a paragraph describing why he/she feels that way.

2. Unsigned, the papers are given to the teacher. After all have participated, a class discussion is held.

CAREER SEARCH

Directions for making activity

1 The name of the activity is placed on the cover page.

2 A grid is drawn on the right center page. Several careers are printed in the squares. They are written vertically, horizontally or diagonally–either forward or backward. The remaining squares are filled in randomly with any letters.

3 The names of the careers listed in the squares may be listed on the left center page. This is optional.

4 The folder is then laminated.

5 A worksheet with a similar grid is provided.

Look for these careers:

- sales
- cook
- doctor
- mechanic
- lawyer
- pilot
- dancer

S	K	J	H	B	V	C	L
R	A	D	O	C	T	O	R
W	L	L	S	U	I	O	T
Y	V	A	E	X	E	K	M
Z	D	W	Q	S	W	P	O
Y	A	Y	X	M	G	T	L
U	N	E	M	F	H	O	U
S	C	R	T	Y	Z	L	X
M	E	C	H	A	N	I	C
D	R	Z	T	V	X	P	P

2 & 3

Directions for use

1. The child fills in the names of careers on his/her worksheet grid matching those found on the folder grid.

2. An alternative method is for the child to copy all the letters found on the folder grid on the worksheet, making sure they are in the same position. Then, outlines are made around each career that is found.

Suggestion: *Two or three CAREER SEARCH folders may be offered at the same time, each listing different careers.*

Grid pattern for CAREER SEARCH

S	K	J	H	B	V	C	L
R	A	D	O	C	T	O	R
W	L	L	S	U	I	O	T
Y	V	A	E	X	E	K	M
Z	D	W	Q	S	W	P	O
Y	A	Y	X	M	G	T	L
U	N	E	M	F	H	O	U
S	C	R	T	Y	Z	L	X
M	E	C	H	A	N	I	C
D	R	Z	T	V	X	P	P

CITY SEARCH

Directions for making activity

1 The name of the activity is placed on the cover page.

2 A grid is drawn on the right center page. The names of several city places are printed in the square. They are written vertically, horizontally or diagonally–either forward or backward. The remaining squares are filled in randomly with any letters.

3 The name of all the city places may be listed on the left center page. This is optional.

4 The folder is then laminated.

5 A worksheet with a similar grid is provided.

2 & 3

Look for these things found in a city.

library
post office
school
hospital
houses
stores
park
zoo

H	O	S	P	I	T	a	L
O	M	W	Y	X	L	I	R
U	Z	F	K	O	B	T	S
S	S	t	O	R	e	s	V
e	L	H	A	T	s	o	P
S	c	R	L	e	B	f	A
S	Y	U	Q	N	U	f	R
Z	B	S	U	B	S	I	K
X	Z	O	O	J	T	C	V
M	G	G	U	H	c	e	W

Directions for use

1. The child fills in the names of city places on his/her worksheet grid, matching those found on the folder grid.

2. An alternative method is for the child to copy all the letters found on the folder grid onto the worksheet, making sure they are in the same position. Then, outlines are made around each city place that is found.

Suggestion: *Several CITY SEARCH folders may be offered at the same time, each listing different places.*

A pattern for a SEARCH grid is given on the following page.

Grid pattern for CITY SEARCH

HELP WANTED

Directions for making activity

1 The name of the activity is placed on the cover page.
2 A list of objects is placed on the center pages. Each object must suggest several jobs related to it.

1

2

Help wanted:

1. car
2. house
3. airplane
4. truck
5. book
6. table
7. stove
8. telephone
9. shoe
10. hospital
11. newspaper
12. magazine
13. pencil
14. bank
15. head
16. paint
17. fruit
18. electricity
19. cotton
20. coffee
21. cigarette
22. typewriter
23. letter
24. horse

Directions for use

1. The child selects one object from the list. He/she then lists jobs related to that object. Reference books may be provided.

For example: The word "telephone" might suggest an operator, a repair person, answering service, switchboard operator, lineman, pollster, clerk in telephone store, information, printer of telephone books, advertiser in yellow pages, designer of telephones, etc.

SHOPPING SPREE

Directions for making activity

1 The name of the activity is placed on the cover page.

2 Cut-outs of items and their costs are pasted on the center pages. Use newspapers or magazines.

3 A limited amount of spending money is indicated somewhere on the center page.

4 Paper and pencils are provided.

Directions for use

1. Taking into consideration the amount of money allowed for spending, the child lists all the things he/she would buy and totals the cost.

Suggestion: *Several file folders similar to this may be offered, each listing a different variety of items.*

COPY THE OATH

Directions for making activity

1 The name of the activity is placed on the cover page.

2 An oath, a famous speech or any part of a well-known document is printed or typed and pasted on the right center page.

3 The name of the oath is typed and pasted on the left center page.

4 The folder is then laminated.

2 & 3

Oath that is taken by the President of the United States as he is sworn into office.

I do solemnly swear that I will faithfully execute the Office of President of the United States and will, to the best of my ability, preserve, protect and defend the Constitution of the United States.

Directions for use

1. Students are required to copy the oath using either manuscript or cursive writing.

Suggestions *for other oaths, speeches, etc. to be used:*
   The Oath of Allegiance to the United States
   The pledge of Allegiance to the flag
   The Hippocratic Oath
   The Gettysburg address
   The Preamble to the Constitution of the United States

SPORTS QUIZ

Directions for making quiz

1 The name of the quiz is placed on the cover page.

2 Ten statements about sports are printed on the center pages. Each statement is missing a key word. The number of dashes for each missing word indicates the number of letters it contains.

3 Numbered answer sheets are provided.

1

SPORTS   QUIZ

1. The ------- is the third man in a boxing ring.
2. An ------ is the judge in a baseball game.
3. A puck is used in ------.
4. Love is a score in ------.
5. There are --- -------yards in the length of a football field.
6. Slam dunk is a shot made in ----------.
7. Swimming up and back is called a ---.
8. What a way to play -------, said the Queen of Hearts.
9. A field goal counts for ----- points in football.
10. ----means get out of the way in golf.

2

Directions for use

1. Children fill in the missing words on the answer sheets.

BASEBALL

Directions for making quiz

1 The name of the quiz is placed on the cover page.

2 Ten statements about BASEBALL are printed on the center pages. Each statement is missing a key word. The number of dashes used in each missing word indicates the number of letters it contains.

3 Numbered answer sheets are provided.

BASEBALL

1. There are – – – – players on each team.
2. What the – – – – – – says, goes.
3. The – – – – – fielder plays in front of and to the side of the batter.
4. – – – – – – three means you're out.
5. A mask is worn by the – – – – – – –.
6. Everyone stretches at the – – – – – – – inning.
7. A – – – – drive is a ball that is hit and it travels fast on the ground between the bases.
8. A bad pitch is a – – – –.
9. There are – – – – innings.
10. Seats that are not choice are called – – – – – – – – –.

Directions for use

1. Children fill in the missing words on the answer sheets.

Suggestion: *Other folder games similar to this one may be prepared for sports such as soccer, football, basketball, tennis, golf, etc.*

SPORTS SEARCH

Directions for making activity

1 The sports section of the newspaper is pasted on the cover page of the folder.

2 A pocket is constructed on the right center page.

3 Cards, each containing a descriptive word such as: score, win, lose, reward, trouble, etc. are placed in the pocket.

4 The folder is then laminated.

5 The teacher saves the sports pages in the newspaper for several days and places them on the folder games table.

6 Lined notebook paper or lined worksheets are provided.

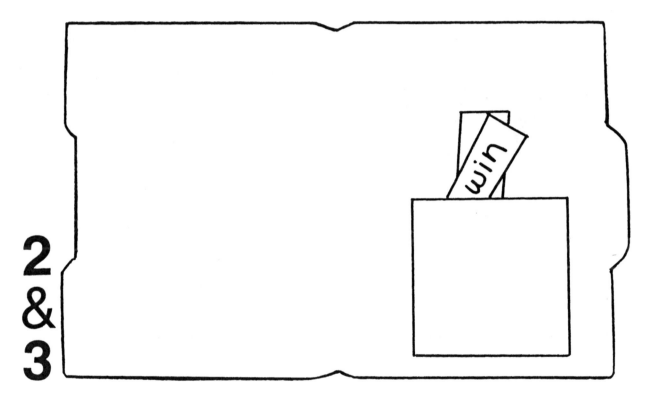

Directions for use

1. Three or four students may participate at one time.

2. Each student selects a word-card and searches through the sports pages to find synonyms for the word.

3. The student lists the synonyms on his/her paper.

TRIVIA–Where Are These Famous Buildings?

Directions for making activity

1 The name of the activity is placed on the cover page.

2 A dozen or more famous buildings are listed on the center pages.

3 Paper and pencils are provided.

1

2

WHERE   ARE   THESE   FAMOUS BUILDINGS?

1. Taj Mahal
2. Westminster Abbey
3. The Kremlin
4. The Parthenon
5. The White House
6. The Palace at Versailles
7. Machu Picchu
8. The Leaning Tower of Pisa
9. The Great Pyramids of Gizeh
10. Buckingham Palace
11. Mayan Ruins in Yucatan
12. Mosque of Suleiman I
13. The palace in the Forbidden City
14. The Opera House in Sydney
15. The Guggenheim Museum of Art
16. Shoënbrunn Palace

Directions for use

1. Students write the answers on their papers and, when finished, hand them to the teacher. Encyclopedias may be used.

2. After all have participated, the answers may be discussed by the entire class.

Suggestion: *Three or four TRIVIA folder activities may be presented at the same time. Children have the option of working one or more of the activities.*

Further ideas for TRIVIA games are given on the following page.

FAIRY TALE TRIVIA

1. The fairy godmother changed the pumpkin into what?
2. Who crossed over the bridge to greener pastures?
3. Who let down her hair?
4. What happened to Rumplestiltskin?
5. What did the little pigs use to build their houses?
6. Why was Jack's mother angry with him?
7. Was the ugly duckling smaller or larger than the other ducklings?
8. Which witch did Dorothy kill?
9. What was Mary Poppins?
10. Who was Christopher Robin?
11. Who were the "lost boys"?
12. What seven things did the little tailor kill in one blow?
13. What is a gnome?
14. What is a troll?

WHAT MISTAKES DID THESE PEOPLE MAKE?

1. Richard Nixon
2. Icarus
3. Benedict Arnold
4. Elvis Presley
5. Billy the Kid
6. General Custer
7. King George III
8. Wrong Way Corrigan
9. Napoleon
10. Louis XVI and Marie Antoinette
11. Romeo and Juliet
12. John Sutter
13. Vidkun Quisling
14. John DeLorean
15. Neville Chamberlain
16. Pandora

More TRIVIA Games

Other TRIVIA games might include Bible questions, famous people, important newspapers, etc.

NOTES

NOTES

NOTES

NOTES